MW01639933

A MOTHER'S YEAR

compiled by

Helen Russ Stough

Fleming H. Revell Company
Old Tappan, New Jersey

By this little token I must express my deepest gratitude and appreciation to that dearest companion,—husband, and lover always, whose interest, encouragement and willing assistance have made this little volume possible.

This is an exact reproduction of a book published by the Fleming H. Revell Company in 1905.

ISBN 0-8007-1437-7

Published by Fleming H. Revell Company
Old Tappan, New Jersey 07675

Printed in the United States of America

ACKNOWLEDGMENT

In presenting this little book, I desire to make very grateful acknowledgment to those who have made it possible; to the owners of copyrights, whether author or publisher, for the privilege of quoting from copyrighted works:

To President Theodore Roosevelt.
To Mr. Joaquin Miller.
To Mr. E. S. Martin.
To Mr. Allen Ayrault Green.
To Mr. Edwin Markham.
To Mr. James Whitcomb Riley.
To Mrs. Margaret E. Sangster.
To Miss Elizabeth Harrison.
To Rev. Sydney Strong.
To Rev. Harry Edward Mills.
To Mr. Patterson Du Bois.
To Mrs. Mary Riley Smith.
To Mr. Frank L. Stanton.
To Bobbs-Merrill Co., for James Whitcomb Riley's poems.
To Baker-Taylor Co., for Rev. Theodore Cuyler's "Recollections."
To D. C. Heath & Company, publishers of the American edition of Malleson's "Early Training of Children."
To Longmans, Green & Company for Ennes Richmond's "Mind of a Child."

To Little, Brown & Co., for quotations from Helen Hunt Jackson and Susan Coolidge.

To Thomas Y. Crowell & Co., for quotations from J. R. Miller's books.

To Mr. John Brisben Walker, for poem by Joaquin Miller, copyright by Cosmopolitan Publishing Co., 1904.

To Tandy-Wheeler Publishing Co., for stanzas from Eugene Field's "Little Book of Tribune Verses."

To American Mother Company, for Mary Wood-Allen, M. D., and Gabrielle E. Jackson's quotations.

To the *Ladies Home Journal*, for Edith Livingston Smith's poem, "Motherhood."

To the *Delineator*, for Agnes Surbridge's "Evolution of a Club Woman."

To McClure, Phillips & Co., for selections from "Heart of My Heart," by Ellis Meredith.

To Harper Bros., for quotations from "The Morning Glow," by Roy Rolfe Gilson, and "The Luxury of Children," by E. S. Martin.

To *Harper's Weekly*, for "The Lost Santa Claus," by Kathryn Jarboe.

To the *Century* Co., for poem by Miss Ethel M. Kelley.

To the Macmillan Co., for quotations from "The People of the Whirlpool," by the author of "The Garden of a Commuter's Wife."

To Charles Scribner's Sons, for quotations from J. G. Holland, and from "The White Bird," by James M. Barrie, and Eugene Field's poems.

The selections from the writings of Henry Wadsworth Longfellow and Kate Douglas Wiggin; also from J. T. Trowbridge and Phœbe Cary, are used by permission and by special arrangement with Houghton, Mifflin & Company, the authorized publishers of the works of these authors.

INTRODUCTION

"A Mother's Year!" How like to each other are the days of it, only a mother knows! The same duties, perplexities, trials and joys! And the great temptation is to sink one's self in the weariness of it and lose the beauties. In all the ways men have to go, no path reaches a higher goal, or goes by a more beautiful way, than the mother's.

It is because I have known the way, the little hindering obstacles, and, as well, the beauty and divinity of the mission, that I have gathered together these bits of inspiration and cheer for each day. May they keep us in remembrance. I know how small a cloud can hide the beautiful vision. And we must not lose the vision,—our wonderful partnership with God.

May these verses, from those who have had the heart to feel and the words to speak, help to give our day a loftier plane, our life a sweeter tone and our eternity a greater triumph.

HELEN RUSS STOUGH.

A MOTHER'S YEAR

A partnership with God is Motherhood,
What strength, what purity, what self-control;
What love, what wisdom shall belong to her
Who helps God fashion an immortal soul.

The Month of January

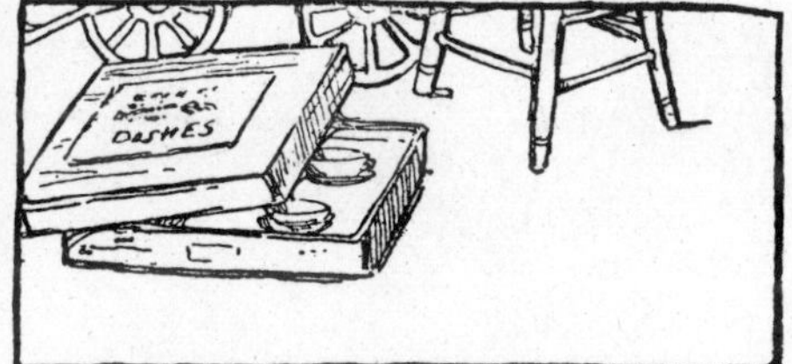

A MOTHER'S YEAR

January First

Blessed be children! Year by year
They appear,
Filling the humblest home with cheer.
Now a daughter and now a son,
One by one
They are cradled, they creep, they walk, they run.

Sons and daughters until, behold!
Young and old,
A Jacob's ladder with steps of gold!
A ladder of little heads! each fair
Head a stair
For the angels that visit the parent pair!

Blessed be childhood! even its chains
Are our gains!
Welcome and blessed with all the pains,

Losses, and upward vanishings
Of light wings,
With all the sorrow and toil it brings,
All burdens that ever those small feet bore
To our door,—
Blessed and welcome forevermore!

—J. T. Trowbridge.

January Second

There came to port last Sunday night
The queerest little craft,
Without an inch of rigging on,—
I looked, and looked, and laughed.
It was so singular that she
Should cross the unknown water,
And moor herself right in my room,—
My daughter, oh, my daughter!

Ring out, wild bells,—and tame ones, too,—
Ring out the lover's moon,
Ring in the little worsted socks,
Ring in the bib and spoon.
Ring out the muse, ring in the nurse,
Ring in the milk and water;
Away with paper, pen and ink,—
My daughter, oh, my daughter

—Anon.

January Third

The woman's task is not easy,—no task worth doing is easy,—but in doing it, and when she has done it, there shall come to her the highest and holiest joy known to mankind; and having done it, she shall have the reward prophesied in Scripture; for her husband and her children, yes, and all people who realize that her work lies at the foundation of all national happiness and greatness, shall rise up and call her blessed.

—*Theodore Roosevelt.*

January Fourth

Perhaps there are tenderer, sweeter things
  Somewhere in this sun-bright land,
But I thank the Lord for His blessings,
  And the clasp of a little hand.

—*Frank L. Stanton.*

Every child walks into existence through the golden gate of love.

—*Henry Ward Beecher.*

How difficult it is to know one's children well; to develop and train the characters according to their different peculiarities and requirements.

—*Princess Alice of Hesse.*

January Fifth

Now I lay me down to sleep —
Don't want to sleep; I want to think.
I didn't mean to spill that ink;
I only meant to softly creep
Under the desk and be a bear —
'Tain't 'bout the spankin' that I care.

I s'pose if I'd cried a lot
An' choked all up like sister does,
An' acted sadder than I wuz,
An' sobbed about the "naughty spot,"
She'd said, "He sha'n't be whipped; he sha'n't,"
An' kissed me—but somehow, I can't.

But I don't think it's fair a bit
That when she talks and talks at you,
An' you wait patient till she's through,
An' start to tell your side of it,
She says, "Now that'll do, my son;
I've heard enough;" 'fore you've begun.

'F I should die before I wake,—
Maybe I ain't got any soul;
Maybe there's only just a hole
Where't ought to be—there's such an ache
Down there somewhere! She seemed to think
That I just loved to spill that ink.

—*Ethel M. Kelly.*

January Sixth

Once I wanted to let my light shine,—but that is very long ago. Now I want to hide it behind the drawn curtains of my home, whatever light there is, just enough to see to read the faces of my loved ones. My hands are too tired to hold a torch on high, but they can light a candle in a nursery. I think all my hopes and ambitions are to be realized in the boy.

—Ellis Meredith.

January Seventh

It is not telling a child what to do, but showing him how to do it and seeing that it is done, taking care that the advice or command we give is put into practice and adopted as a habit.

—Andrew Murray.

And when the sun at break of day
Crept in upon His hair,
I think it must have left a ray
Of unseen glory there,
A kiss of love on that little brow
For the thorns that it must wear.

—Albert Bigelow Paine.

January Eighth

Perhaps no one ever praised a woman more gracefully in a sentence than Steele when he said of Lady Elisabeth Hastings that "to know her was a liberal education"; but every woman may feel as she improves herself that she is not only laying in a store of happiness for herself, but also raising and blessing him whom she would most wish to see happy and good.

—*Sir John Lubbock.*

January Ninth

Thus our words from day to day
Echoed are in "baby's say."
And our spirit, harsh or kind,
Mars or mends the infant mind.

All our manners, chaste or rude
By the babe are understood,
Guard well, then, the plastic mind;
"As the twig's bent, the tree's inclined."

—*S. D. Horine.*

January Tenth

Ah, what if they should? What if your boy or
 mine
Should cross o'er the threshold which marks out the
 line
'Twixt virtue and vice, 'twixt pureness and sin,
And leave all his innocent boyhood within?
Oh, what if they should, because you and I,
While the days and the months and the years hurry
 by,
Are too busy with cares and with life's fleeting joys
To make 'round our hearthstones a place for the
 boys?

—*Boston Transcript.*

January Eleventh

When the house keeps in order all day,
 No chairs overturned on the floor,
No rocking-horse left in the way,
 No wagon obstructing the door;
No fragments of cookies or cake,
 No traces of frolicsome play,
The heartstrings of motherhood break
 When the house keeps in order all day.

—*Harry Edward Mills.*

January Twelfth

Little girlie-girl, of you
  Still forever I am dreaming,—
Laughing eyes of limpid blue—
  Tresses glimmering and gleaming
Like glad waters, running over
Shelving shallows, rimmed with clover,
  Trembling where the eddies whirl,
  Gurgling "Little Girly-Girl!"

For your name it came to me
  Down the brink of brooks that brought it
Out of Paradise,—and we,—
  Love and I,—we, leaning, caught it
From the ripples romping nigh us,
And the bubbles bumping by us
  Over shoals of pebbled pearl,
  Lilting "Little Girly-Girl!"

—*James Whitcomb Riley.*

January Thirteenth

Heavenly music of the first cry! Sacred voice of life, first sound of the poem of a heart, thou echo of God's word! What sound is like unto thee? Yes, it is so: the cry of the baby is music! When it is still, especially in the night, one is uneasy; one longs for this primitive expression of that little being, and is consoled, enraptured, when the helpless creature breaks into loud wails, and says to us, "I live! Give me what I need!" Oh, cry of the baby in the night, nightingale song for mother and father!

—*Semmig.*

January Fourteenth

Two faces o'er a cradle bent;
  Two hands above the head were locked,
  These pressed each other while they rocked,
These watched a life that love had sent,
  O solemn hour!
  O hidden power.

Two parents by the evening fire;
  The red light fell about their knees
  On heads that rose by slow degrees
Like buds upon the lily spire;
  O patient life!
  O tender strife!

—*George Eliot.*

January Fifteenth

I heard their prayers and kissed their sleepy eyes,
  And tucked them in all warm from feet to head,
To wake again with morning's glad sunrise,—
  Then came where he lay dead.
Those other children to men have grown,—
  Strange, hurried men, who give me passing thought,
They go their ways. No longer now my own.
  Without me they have wrought.
So when night comes, and seeking mother's knee,
  Tired childish feet turn home at eventide,
I fold him close,—the little child that's left to me,
  My little lad who died.

—*Anon.*

January Sixteenth

I think it must somewhere be written that the virtues of mothers shall, occasionally, be visited on their children, as well as the sins of their fathers.

—*Charles Dickens.*

Love through all deeps of her spirit lies bared to me
  Oft as I look on the face of her child.

—*Anon.*

January Seventeenth

Place a spray in thy belt, or a rose on thy stand,
When thou settest thyself to a commonplace seam;
Its beauty will brighten the work in thy hand,
Its fragrance will sweeten each dream.

When the task thou performest is irksome and long,
Or thy brain is perplexed by doubt or by fear,
Fling open the window and let in the song
God hath taught to the bird for thy cheer.

—*Anon.*

January Eighteenth

The problem is to train up a child in the way he should grow. Grow he will in any case; what we want is, so to control the circumstances that call forth his activity that he shall grow as straight as possible, as much as possible in as many directions as possible, but as harmoniously as possible.

—*James Ward.*

I hold it a religious duty,
To love and worship children's beauty;
They've least the taint of earthly clod,
They're freshest from the hand of God.

—*Campbell.*

January Nineteenth

But it is blessedness! A year ago
  I did not see it as I do to-day;
We are so dull and thankless, and so slow
  To catch the sunshine till it slips away.
And now it seems surpassing strange to me,
  That while I wore the badge of motherhood,
I did not kiss more oft and tenderly
  The little child that brought me only good.

—*Mary Riley Smith.*

January Twentieth

The tear that slowly gathers as she gazes, is not grief that the bloom has faded from my cheek, but the sweet consciousness that it can never fade from my heart; and as her eyes fall upon her work again, or the children climb into her lap to hear the old fairy tales they already know by heart, my wife Prue is dearer to me than the sweetheart of those days long ago.

—*George William Curtis.*

January Twenty-first

He sleeps, my darling baby boy,
  My life, my hope, my sweetest joy!
How like a budding, blushing rose
  His tiny mouth, now in repose!
How white his chubby, dimpled fists,
  How plump and creased his baby wrists!
His little neck, how soft and sleek,
  His chubby legs, how childish weak!
How sweet to gaze on baby's face
  And dream of future manhood days.

—*Eugene Field.*

January Twenty-second

Gods sends children for another purpose than merely to keep up the race,—to enlarge our hearts, to make us unselfish and full of kindly sympathies and affections; to give our souls higher aims and to call out all our faculties, to extend enterprise and exertion; to bring round our firesides bright faces and happy smiles, and loving, tender hearts. My soul blesses the great Father every day that He has gladdened the earth with little children.

—*Mary Howitt.*

January Twenty-third

Who can tell what a baby thinks?
Who can follow the gossamer links
  By which the mannikin feels his way
Out from the shore of the great unknown,
Blind, and wailing and alone,
  Into the light of day?
Out from the shore of the unknown sea,
Tossing in pitiful agony,—
Of the unknown sea that reels and rolls,
Specked with the barks of little souls,
Barks that were launched on the other side,
And slipped from Heaven on an ebbing tide!

—*J. G. Holland.*

January Twenty-fourth

The child's grief throbs against the round of its little heart as heavily as the man's sorrow, and the one finds as much delight in his kite or drum as the other in striking the springs of enterprise or soaring on the wings of fame.

—*E. H. Chapin.*

Children are God's apostles, day by day,
Sent forth to preach of love, and hope and peace,
Nor will thy babe its mission leave undone.

—*James Russell Lowell.*

January Twenty-fifth

I will pour My Spirit upon thy seed,
And My blessing upon thine offspring;
And they shall spring up as among the grass,
As willows by the water-courses.

—*Isaiah 44:3, 4.*

Pointing to such, well might Cornelia say,
When the rich casket shown in bright array,
"These are my jewels!" Well, of such as he,
When Jesus spake, well might the language be,
"Suffer these little ones to come to Me!"

—*Samuel Rogers.*

January Twenty-sixth

But Jesus said, Suffer little children and forbid them not, to come unto Me: for of such is the kingdom of heaven.

—*Matthew 19:14.*

It was long years ago that He uttered
This message so tender and sweet,
And women were crowding about Him
And laying their babes at His feet.
He looked with a gentle compassion
On the mothers who knelt at His knee,
And He comforted them with this saying,
"Let the little ones come unto Me."

—*Mary Riley Smith.*

January Twenty-seventh

If I were to choose among all the gifts and qualities that which, on the whole, makes life pleasanter, I should select the love of children. No circumstances can render this world wholly a solitude to one who has this possession.

—*Thomas Wentworth Higginson.*

"Above all our sympathy and regard are due to the struggling wives among those whom Abraham Lincoln called the plain people, and whom he so loved and trusted; for the lives of these women are often led on the lonely heights of quiet, self-sacrificing heroism."

—*Theodore Roosevelt.*

January Twenty-eighth

A sweeter shape
Stands in its place. O blest maternity!
Hushed on her bosom, in a light embrace,
Her baby sleeps, wrapped in its long white robe;
And as the flame, with soft, auroral sweeps,
Illuminates the pair, how like they seem,
O Virgin Mother! To thyself and Thine!

—*J. G. Holland.*

January Twenty-ninth

Why should we be astonished at the warped, cold, unhappy, suspicious natures we see about us, when we reflect upon the number of unwished-for, unwelcomed children in the world,—children who at best were never loved until they were seen and known, and were often grudged their being from the moment they began to be. I wonder if sometimes a starved, crippled, agonized human body and soul does not cry out, "Why, O man, O woman;—why, being what I am, have you suffered me to be?"

—Kate D. Wiggin.

January Thirtieth

It was not by the birth of Mary's Son that God's kingdom was to come. Believing parents may look upon their children as the stones of the great temple of which Jesus was the corner stone.

—Andrew Murray.

Love is the Holy Ghost within;
   Hate, the unpardonable sin!
Who preaches otherwise than this,
   Betrays his Master with a kiss.

—H. W. Longfellow.

January Thirty-first

Aunt Eleanor wears such diamonds!
  Shiny and gay and grand,
Some on her neck and some in her hair,
  And some on her pretty hand.
One day I asked my mamma
  Why she never wore them, too;
She laughed and said, as she kissed my eyes,
  "My jewels are here, bright blue.
They laugh and dance and beam and smile,
  So lovely all the day,
And never like Aunt Eleanor's go
  In a velvet box to stay.
Hers are prisoned in bands of gold,
  But mine are free as air,
Set in a bonny, dimpled face,
  And shadowed with shining hair!

—*Eugene Field.*

The Month of February

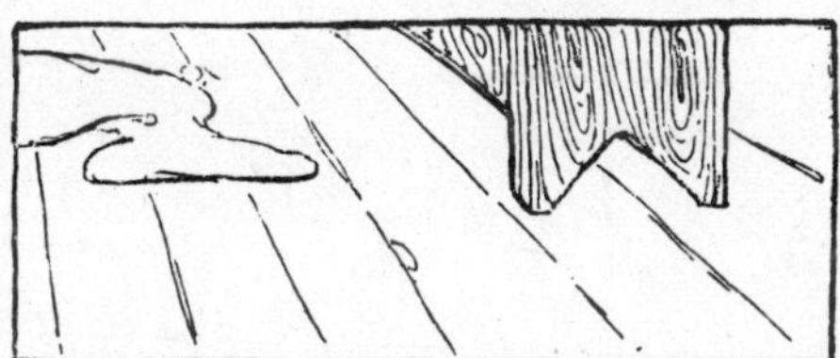

February First

My baby boy, I sing of thee
Because thou art like song to me.
Thy joys and fears, thy smiles and tears,
  Are rythmic in their rising.
Thy pantomimes, like tropes and rhymes,
  Are full of sweet surprising.
A little lyric bit thou art;
A drama quickens in thy heart,
    Concealed forsooth;
But through thy deep soul-magic
    I see the truth.
  Thy comedies are tragic.

—Patterson Du Bois.

February Second

For the mother is and must be, whether she knows it or not, the greatest, strongest and most lasting teacher her children have. Other influences come and go, but hers is continual; and by the opinion men have of women we can generally judge of the sort of mother they had.

—Hannah Whitall Smith.

The constant anxiety about the children is dreadful; and it is not physical ill one dreads for them—it is moral.

—Princess Alice.

February Third

Compared with thy endurance, that of the young man, the athlete, is as weakness; the secret of thy nerves, wonderful even in their weakness, is as great as that of the power of the winds. To display decision, thy opportunities are more frequent than those of the greatest statesmen; thy heroism laughs into insignificance that of fort and field; thou art trained in a school of diplomacy such as the most experienced court cannot furnish. Easier is it to rule a band of savages than to be the successful autocrat of thy little kingdom.

—*John Habberton.*

February Fourth

Sweet has been the charm of childhood on my spirit, throughout my ramble with little Annie! Say not that it has been a waste of precious moments, an idle matter, a babble of childish talk and a reverie of childish imaginations about topics unworthy of a grown man's notice. Has it been merely this? Not so. Not so. As the pure breath of children revives the life of aged men, so is our moral nature revived by their free and simple thoughts, their native feeling, their airy mirth, for little cause or none their grief, soon roused and soon allayed.

—*Nathaniel Hawthorne.*

February Fifth

Ten little heads have found their sweetest rest
  Upon the pillow of her loving breast;
The world is wide; yet nowhere does it keep
  So safe a haven, so secure a rest.

'Tis counted something great to be a queen,
  And bend a kingdom to a woman's will.
To be a mother such as mine, I ween,
  Is something better and more noble still.

—*Mary Riley Smith.*

February Sixth

Love is kind and suffers long;
Love is meek and thinks no wrong;
Love than death itself more strong,—
  Therefore give us love.

—*Anon.*

The mother's heart is the child's schoolroom.

—*Henry Ward Beecher.*

February Seventh

Little Mistress Sans-Merci
Fareth world-wide, fancy free;
  Trotteth cooing to and fro,
    And her cooing is command;
  Never ruled there yet, I trow,
    Mightier despot in the land.
And my heart it lieth where
Mistress Sans-Merci doth fare.

Little Mistress Sans-Merci
Hath become so dear to me
  That I count as passing sweet
    All the pain her moods impart,
  And I bless the little feet
    That go trampling on my heart;
Ah, how lonely life would be
But for little Sans-Merci!

—*Eugene Field.*

(From "With Trumpet and Drum," by courtesy of the publishers, Charles Scribner's Sons.)

February Eighth

Into the woman's keeping is committed the destiny of the generations to come after us. In bringing up your children you mothers must remember that while it is essential to be loving and tender, it is no less essential to be wise and firm. If you mothers through weakness bring up your sons to be selfish and to think only of themselves, you will be responsible for much sadness among the women who are to be their wives in the future. If you let your daughters grow up idle, perhaps under the mistaken impression that as you yourselves have had to work hard they shall know only enjoyment, you are preparing them to be useless to others and burdens to themselves. Teach boys and girls alike that they are not to look forward to lives spent in avoiding difficulties, but to lives spent in overcoming difficulties.

—*Theodore Roosevelt.*

February Ninth

Let us believe that God always gives grace proportioned to the duty He imposes. Let the believing parent live and act,—and pray *with* and *for* his children, as one to whom the ark (home) and its salvation is indeed the one aim and joy of life, and who is assured that his children are meant of God to be there with him.

—*Andrew Murray.*

February Tenth

I have had compliments, now and then,
From grown-up women and grown-up men;
Some were commonplace, some were new,
Never was one of them rung so true,
Never was one seemed half so real;
Baby compared me to his ideal.

—*S. St. G. Lawrence.*

February Eleventh

I have a son, a third sweet son, his age I cannot tell,
For they reckon not, by years and months where he has gone to dwell.
To us, for fourteen anxious months, his infant smiles were given,
And then he bade farewell to earth and went to live in Heaven.

I cannot tell what form is his, what looks he weareth now,
Nor guess how bright a glory crowns his shining seraph brow.
But I know (for God hath told me this) that he is now at rest,
Where other blessed infants be,—on their Saviour's loving breast.

—*James Moultrie.*

February Twelfth

All that I am or hope to be I owe to my mother.

—*Abraham Lincoln.*

Kneel, little laddie, at my side;
There's no defence like this;
An evening prayer in childish trust,
And let him scoff who may;—
A daily prayer to God above,
A gentle mother's kiss,
Will keep my little laddie safe,
However long the day.

—*Anon.*

February Thirteenth

Oh, mothers, so weary, discouraged,
Worn out with the cares of the day,
You often grow cross and impatient,
Complain of the noise and the play.
For the day brings so many vexations,
So many things going amiss;
But, mothers, whatever may vex you,
Send the children to bed with a kiss.

—*Anon.*

February Fourteenth

Baby came toddling up to my knee,
His chubby features all aglow,
" Dess I'se doin' to be 'oor beau,
See what oo' dat from me!"
A valentine from baby boy!
A crumpled sheet and a homely scrawl,
In a baby-hand—that was all—
Yet it filled my heart with joy.

Broken my heart and white my hair,
And my mother eyes are used to weep,
My little boy is fast asleep
In the churchyard over there.
What shall be mamma's valentine?
The spirit touch of the baby hand,
A baby voice from the spirit-land,
Singing a song divine.

—*Eugene Field.*

February Fifteenth

Love childhood, encourage its sports, its pleasures, its amiable instincts. Who of you has not sometimes looked back with regret on that age when a smile was ever on the lips, when the soul was ever at peace?

—*Jean J. Rousseau.*

What are Raphael's Madonnas but the shadow of a mother's love fixed in permanent outlines forever?

—*Thomas Wentworth Higginson.*

February Sixteenth

"An ounce of mother," says the Spanish proverb, "is worth a pound of clergy."

—*Thomas Wentworth Higginson*

Mother-sense is a subtle matter. Some women lack it who have the most admirable theories about raising children, and the most outspoken views as to the errors and delinquencies of other mothers; therefore, when you are looking for it, if you want to be particularly sagacious, look not at the mother but at the children. The proof of the mothering lies in them; but even that is not infallible, for sometimes a good deputy does wonders.

—*E. S. Martin.*

February Seventeenth

Mother, I see you with your nursery light,
Leading your babies, all in white,
To their sweet rest;
Christ, the Good Shepherd, carries mine to-night,
And that is best.

You know over yours may hang even now
Pain and disease, whose fulfilling slow
Naught can arrest;
Mine in God's gardens run to and fro,
And that is best.

But grief is selfish, and I cannot see
Always, why I should so stricken be,
More than the rest;
But I know that as well as for them for me,
God did the best.

—*Helen Hunt.*

February Eighteenth

Whosoever shall humble himself as this little child, the same is greatest in the kingdom of heaven, and whoso receiveth one such little child in My name receiveth Me.

—*Matthew 18 : 4, 5.*

If a choice must be made between us, I think it is my right to lay down my life for yours. Being your mother, how could I do less? I cannot see that there is any other side to this, but your father could never endure what I can endure. For that matter, reverse the situation, and I know I could not see him suffer, —suffer as I must,—not even for the sake of you, my son, and I understand what is ahead of me better than he can.

—*Ellis Meredith.*

February Nineteenth

" A kiss from my mother made me a painter," said the veteran artist, Benjamin West, after he had won fame and hung his pictures in Royal Academies. When she looked at his first boyish sketch, she praised it; if she had been a silly or sulky parent, she might have said, " Foolish child, don't waste your time on such daubs," and so have quenched the first spark of his ambition.

—*Theodore Cuyler.*

February Twentieth

" Bless your tormenting, honest little heart," I said to myself, " if men trusted God as you do your papa, how little business there'd be for preachers to do."

—*John Habberton.*

A healthy babe, coolly and loosely dressed, judiciously fed, and frequently bathed, will be good and comfortable if it have not too much attention. But when it is liable a dozen times a day to be caught wildly up, bounced and jumped about, smothered with kisses, poked by facetious fingers, and petted until it is thoroughly out of sorts, what can be expected of it? How would fathers and mothers endure the martyrdom to which they allow the babies to be subjected?

—*Margaret Sangster.*

February Twenty-first

Have you tasted of the sweetness
  Of those little dewy lips?
Would you change it for the nectar
  We are told the fairy sips?
That has power to please the senses,
  While the kiss of children brings
Thoughts of heaven, and oft a longing
  For the purer, grander things.

—*Minnette McElheny.*

February Twenty-second

I have known Abraham to the end that he may command his household and his children after him, that they may keep the way of the Lord to do justice and judgment.

—*Genesis 18 : 19.*

Every parent who allows himself the luxury of his children's society may expect to be imitated in such measure as the child approves. Such imitation is obedience, even though it may accord very imperfectly with the word of the parental command.

—*E. S. Martin.*

February Twenty-third

Lennavan-mo,
Lennavan-mo,
It is only a little wee lass you are, Eilidh-mo-chree,
But as this wee blossom has roots in the depths of the sky,
So you are at one with the Lord of Eternity,—
Bonny wee lass that you are,
My morning star,
Eilidh-mo-chree, Lennavan-mo,
Lennavan-mo.

—*Fiona Macleod.*

February Twenty-fourth

In the old days there were angels who came and took men by the hand and led them away from the city of destruction. We see no white-winged angels now; but yet men are led away from threatening destruction. A hand is put into theirs, which leads them forth gently towards a calm and bright land, so that they look no more backwards, and the hand may be a little child's.

—*George Eliot.*

February Twenty-fifth

What is the little one thinking about?
Very wonderful things, no doubt!
        Unwritten history!
        Unfathomed mystery!
Yet he laughs and cries, and eats and drinks,
And chuckles and crows, and nods and winks,
   As if his head were as full of kinks
   And curious riddles as any sphinx!
        Warped by colic and wet by tears,
        Punctured by pins and tortured by fears,
Our little nephew will lose two years;
        And he'll never know
        Where the summers go;
He need not laugh, for he'll find it so!

—*J. G. Holland.*

(From "Bittersweet," published by Charles Scribner's Sons.)

February Twenty-sixth

Why is it that so many women are afraid to be left alone with their thoughts between six and seven? I believe, Mary, that when you close David's door softly, there is a gladness in your eyes, and the awe of one who knows that the God to whom little boys say their prayers has a face very like their mother's.

—*J. M. Barrie.*

(From "The Little White Bird," by courtesy of Charles Scribner's Sons, publishers.)

February Twenty-seventh

Heaven help all mothers if they be not really dears, for their boy will certainly know it in that strange short hour of the day, when every mother stands revealed before her little son. That dread hour ticks between six and seven; when children go to bed later, the revelation has ceased to come. He is lapt in for the night now and lies quietly there, madam, with great, mysterious eyes fixed upon his mother. He is summing up your day.

—*J. M. Barrie.*

(From "The Little White Bird," by courtesy of Charles Scribner's Sons, publishers.)

February Twenty-eighth

From over the hills of Judea,
Down through the long line of the years,
That voice of ineffable sweetness
Still comforts the mother's sad tears.
Oh, Heart that has bled for our sorrows,
O Voice that can quiet the sea!
Come often to me with Thy whisper:
"Let the little ones come unto Me."

O mothers, whose children are lying
Out under the snow and the rain,
Let the beautiful words of the Master
Give ease to your sorrow and pain!
He holds the bright heads on His bosom,
He gathers them close to His knee,
And tenderly still He is saying,
"Let the little ones come unto Me."

—*Mary Riley Smith.*

February Twenty-ninth

Hold diligent converse with thy children! Have them
Morning and evening round thee; love thou them,
And win their love in these rare, beauteous years,
For only while the short-lived dream of childhood
Lasts are they thine;—no longer!

—***Anon.***

The Month of March

March First

A funny little chin,
  And a funny little nose,
A funny little grin,
  Ten funny little toes.
Two funny little eyes,
  And funny little hands,
How funnily he tries
  To give his wee commands.

A funny little sigh,
  A funny little head,
That funnily will try
  To miss the time for bed.
A funny little peep
  From funny eyes that gleam,
A funny little sleep,
  A funny little dream.

—*Eugene Field.*

March Second

You sail and you seek for the Fortunate Isles,
The old Greek Isles of the yellow-bird's song?
Then steer straight on through the watery miles,
Straight on, straight on, and you can't go wrong,
Nay, not to the left, nay, not to the right,
But on, straight on, and the isles are in sight,
The Fortunate Isles where the yellow-birds sing
And life lies girt with a golden ring.

These Fortunate Isles they are not so far,
They lie within reach of the lowliest door,
You can see them gleam by the twilight star;
You can hear them sing by the moon's white shore—
Nay, never look back! Those levelled gravestones
They were landing-steps; they were steps unto thrones
Of glory for souls that have sailed before,
And have set white feet on the fortunate shore.

And what are the names of the Fortunate Isles?
Why, Duty and Love and a large Content,
Lo! these are the isles of the watery miles,
That God let down from the firmament.
Lo! Duty and Love and a true man's Trust;
Your forehead to God, though your feet in the dust;
Lo! Duty and Love, and a sweet babe's smiles,
And these, O friend, are the Fortunate Isles.

—*Joaquin Miller.*

March Third

God bless their dear, patient souls! If men and women brought to bear on the thwartings and vexations of their daily lives and their relations with each other, one-hundredth part of the sweet acquiescence and brave endurance which average children show, under the average management of average parents, this world would be a much pleasanter place to live in than it is.

—*Helen Hunt Jackson.*

March Fourth

"It's only a little grave," they said,
"Only a child's that's dead;"
And so they carelessly turned away
From the mound the spade had made that day.
Ah! They did not know how deep a shade
That little grave in our home had made.

'Tis a little grave; but oh, have care!
For world-wide hopes are buried there;
And ye, perhaps, in coming years,
May see, like her, through blinding tears,
How much of light, how much of joy,
Is buried with an only boy.

—*Anon.*

March Fifth

Love, sowing in the heart of man the sweet harvest of desire, mixes the sweetest and most beautiful things together.

—*Melanippides.*

The hearts of some women tremble like leaves at every breath of love which reaches them, and then are still again. Others, like the ocean, are moved only by the breath of a storm, and not so easily lulled to rest.

—*H. W. Longfellow.*

March Sixth

Quietness is a blessed secret for the wives and mothers in the home. It is impossible for any gentle woman, though her household life be even ideally Christian and happy, to avoid having many experiences that try her sensitive spirit. Nothing but the love on her part that is not provoked, that doth not behave itself unseemly, that can be silent and sweet —not silent and sullen, but silent and sweet,—in any circumstances, can make even holiest wedded life what it should be. Blessed the wife who has learned this lesson!

—*J. R. Miller.*

March Seventh

A father may turn his back on his child, brothers and sisters may become inveterate enemies, husbands may desert their wives; wives, their husbands; but a mother's love endures, through all, in good repute, in bad repute, in the face of the world's condemnation, a mother still loves on and still hopes that her child may turn from his evil ways and repent; still she remembers the infant smiles that once filled her bosom with rapture, the merry laugh, the joyful shout of his childhood, the opening promise of his youth; and she can never be brought to think him all unworthy.

—*Washington Irving.*

March Eighth

The formative period of building character for eternity is in the nursery. The mother is queen of that realm and sways a sceptre more potent than that of kings or priests.

—*Anon.*

By the fireside the light is shining,
The children's arms 'round the parents twining;
From love so sweet, oh, who would roam?
Be it ever so homely, home is home.

—*Dinah M. Muloch.*

March Ninth

The child is father of the man.

—*William Wordsworth.*

Almost any kind of a parent will do at a pinch, except a liar. If we are exceptionally commendable persons, as people go, so much the better for our children, for like not only breeds like but trains like, and "good father," "good child" is a fairly reliable rule, though "good mother," "good child" is a somewhat surer one.

—*E. S. Martin.*

March Tenth

Sail east, sail west, O wanderer,
  In east, in west, you cannot see
Such suns as rise and set in these
  Four little faces round my knee.

Sail east, sail west, dear wanderer!
  God cares for you and cares for me
He knows for which of us 'twas best
  To stay with children round her knee.

—*Helen Hunt Jackson.*

March Eleventh

In the morn of the holy Sabbath,
  I like in the Church to see
Dear little children gathered
  And worshipping there with me,
They sit in the congregation
  With faces grave and sweet,
And the Master looks upon them,—
  His lilies among the wheat.

—*Dr. Mary Wood-Allen.*

March Twelfth

A wife! A mother!—two magical words, comprising the sweetest source of man's felicity. Theirs is the reign of beauty, of love, of reason,—always a reign.

—*Aimi Martin.*

A partnership with God is Motherhood;
  What strength, what purity, what self-control,
What love, what wisdom should belong to her
  Who helps God fashion an immortal soul.

—*Anon.*

March Thirteenth

Only a baby small,
  Dropped from the skies;
Only a laughing face,
  Two sunny eyes.
Only two cherry lips,
  One chubby nose,
Only two little hands,
  Ten little toes.

Only a tender flower,
  Sent us to rear.
Only a life to love,
  While we are here.
Only a baby small,
  Never at rest,
Small, but how dear to us
  God knoweth best.

—*Mattias Barr.*

March Fourteenth

We need love's tender lessons taught
As only weakness can;
God hath His small interpreters,
The child must teach the man.

We wander wide through evil years,
Our eyes of faith grow dim;
But he is freshest from His hands,
And nearest unto Him.

—*J. G. Whittier.*

March Fifteenth

I lay pondering over the vast amount of unused ingenuity that was looked up in millions of children, or employed only to work misery among unsuspecting adults, when I heard light footfalls at my bedside and saw a small shape with a grave face approach and remark, " I wants to come in your bed."

—*John Habberton.*

Always leave home with loving words, for they may be the last.

—*Anon.*

March Sixteenth

Away in a manger,
No crib for His bed,
The Little Lord Jesus
Laid down His sweet head.

The stars in the heaven
Looked down where He lay,
The Little Lord Jesus,
Asleep on the hay.

The cattle are lowing,
The baby awakes,
But Little Lord Jesus,
No crying He makes.

I love Thee, Lord Jesus!
Look down from the sky,
And stay by my cradle
Till morning is nigh.

—*Martin Luther.*

March Seventeenth

The hand that rocks the cradle rules the world.

—*John Gray.*

Favour is deceitful, and beauty is vain ;
But a woman that feareth the Lord, she shall
be praised.
Give her of the fruit of her hands,
And let her works praise her in the gates.

—*Proverbs 31 : 30, 31.*

March Eighteenth

They are idols of hearts and of households ;
They are angels of God in disguise ;
His sunlight still sleeps in their tresses,
His glory still shines in their eyes ;
Those truants from home and from heaven,
They have made me more manly and mild ;
And I know now how Jesus could liken
The kingdom of God to a child.

—*Charles M. Dickenson.*

March Nineteenth

The training of children is a profession where we must know how to lose time in order to gain it.

—*Jean J. Rousseau.*

To try to make a child good by showing him the horrors of evil is as though we were to try to teach a child to love the sunlight by shutting him up in a dark cavern.

—*Ennes Richmond.*

March Twentieth

Young mother, your motherhood is in God's sight a holier and a more blessed thing than you know. Be sure that all the tender interest and solemn thought, all the quiet trust and joyful hope which expectant motherhood calls forth may be sanctified and refined by God's Holy Spirit, and you be united under the overshadowing of His Heavenly grace.

—*Andrew Murray.*

March Twenty-first

The priest, as he looked on, thanked God, in his heart of hearts, for the greatest of blessings, the return of health, and for the sight most beautiful of all His gifts, the sight of a sleeping child.

—*Edward Everett Hale.*

Sleep on, thou fair child, for thy long rough journey is at hand. A little while and thou shalt sleep no more, but thy very dreams shall be mimic battles.—As yet, sleep and waking are one; the fair life's garden rustles infinite around, and everywhere is dewy fragrance and a budding hope.

—*Thomas Carlyle.*

March Twenty-second

If ye then, being evil, know how to give good gifts unto your children, how much more shall your Father which is in heaven give good things to them that ask Him?

Ask, and it shall be given you;
Seek, and ye shall find;
Knock, and it shall be opened unto you;
For every one that asketh, receiveth;
And he that seeketh, findeth;
And to him that knocketh it shall be opened.

—*Matthew 7:11, 7, 8.*

March Twenty-third

But oh! If the tops were not scattered about,
  And the house never echoed to racket and rout;
If forever the rooms were all tidy and neat,
  And one need not brush after wee, muddy feet,
If no one laughed out when the morning was red
  And with kisses went tumbling all tired to bed,
What a wearisome, workaday world, don't you see,
  For all who loved wild little laddies 'twould be,
And I'm happy to think, tho' I shrink like a mouse
  From disorder and din,—there's a boy in the house!

March Twenty-fourth

Out of the darkness, light; out of the chill and dreary atmosphere of failure and regret, clearer sight; a warmer heart, a better life. Our efforts may seem to be in vain when they result in failure, but the failure itself need not be in vain. The responsibility is upon us of making failures serve a good purpose in showing where we have been inexperienced, thoughtless, weak, unjust. Then out of the darkness and cold shall flame forth light and warmth; out of the wrong shall come the right; out of the tears of a child, the smiles of childhood.

—*Patterson Du Bois.*

March Twenty-fifth

A little hand that softly stole
Into my own that day,
When I needed the touch
That I loved so much
To strengthen me on the way.

I've pored o'er many a yellow page
Of ancient wisdom, and have won,
Perchance, a scholar's name,—but sage
Or bard has never taught thy son
Lesson so dear, so fraught with holy truth,
As those his mother's faith shed on his youth.

—*Anon.*

March Twenty-sixth

"Maternal love," like an orange tree, buds and blossoms and bears at once. When a true woman puts her finger for the first time into the tiny hand of her baby and feels that helpless clutch which tightens her very heart-strings, she is born again with the new-born child.

—*Kate D. Wiggin.*

March Twenty-seventh

Smooth back your brown curls, Annie, and let me tie on your bonnet, and we will set forth! What a strange couple to go on their rambles together! One walks in black attire, with a measured step and a heavy brow, with his thoughtful eyes bent down; while the gay little girl trips lightly along as if she were forced to keep hold of my hand lest her feet should dance from the earth. Yet there is sympathy between us. If I pride myself on anything, it is because I have a smile that children love; on the other hand, there are few grown ladies that could entice me from the side of little Annie, for I delight to let my mind go hand in hand with the mind of a sinless child.

—Nathaniel Hawthorne.

March Twenty-eighth

Who cannot find God in the heart of a child will never know Him within cathedral walls.

—Anon.

Earth's creeds may be seventy times seven,
And blood have defiled each creed;
If "of such be the kingdom of heaven,"
It must be heaven indeed.

—Algernon C. Swinburne.

March Twenty-ninth

And she thought, I, too, am an artist,
My life-work here I see;
This sweet, dear face my hand must trace;
I must paint for eternity.
Hence each dark passion shadow!
Pain's deeply graven lines!
Here must be the reflected beauty
That from the pure heart shines.

Alas, that I am but a learner!
So where shall I make me wise,
Or obtain the rare old colours,—
The Master's precious dyes?
I must haste to the fount of beauty,
Must pleadingly kneel at his feet,
And crave, 'mid his wiser scholars,
The humblest pupil's seat.

—*Anon.*

March Thirtieth

Naked on parents' knees, a new-born child,
Weeping thou sat'st, when all around thee smiled;
So live that, sinking to thy last long sleep,
Thou then may'st smile while all around thee weep.

—*Sir William Jones.*

The mother in her office holds the key
Of the soul; and she it is who stamps the coin
Of character, and makes the being, who would be a savage
But for her gentle cares, a Christian man.

—*Anon.*

March Thirty-first

What trifles filled my darling's heart with grief,
What simpler trifles turned it into joy;
A little fall brought tears, a kiss, relief,
He offered scarf and mittens for a toy;
He talked all day about his cherished plan,
To be, when grown, an organ grinder man.

Sleep lays my riper follies by awhile;
Does God recount them then and fondly smile?

—*Harry Edward Mills.*

The Month of

April First

No rubies of red for my lady,
    No jewel that glitters and charms;—
But the light of the skies,
In a little one's eyes,
    And a necklace of two little arms.

Of two little arms that are clinging,
    (Oh ne'er was a necklace like this!)
And the wealth of the world,
And love's sweetness impearled,
    In the joy of a little one's kiss.

A necklace of love for my lady,
    That was linked by the angels above,—
No other but this,
And a tender, sweet kiss,
    That sealeth a little one's love.

—*Frank L. Stanton.*

⚜

April Second

Is there a place holier than the soul of a child?

—Elizabeth Harrison.

The queenliest woman, bravest, best
Of all sweet things beneath the sun?
I say the queenliest is that one—
Seek north or south or east or west,—
Who loves to fold the little frock
And hear the cradle rock and rock.

I say the purest woman, best
Beneath our forty stars, is she
Who loves her spouse most ardently
And rocks the cradle oftenest—
Who rocks and sings and rocks, and then
When birds are nesting, rocks again.

—Joaquin Miller.

April Third

I bring my children up as simply and with as few wants as I can, and above all, teach them to help themselves and others, so as to become independent.

—Princess Alice of Hesse.

Children are the hands by which we take hold of heaven.

—Henry Ward Beecher.

April Fourth

I don't know any reason why a man should never have the fun of giving his baby a bath, until he takes his boy for his first swimming lesson. And on the other hand, they make too much of their natural virtues, lay too much stress on their emotional natures, claim a monopoly of feeling and sentiment, as if men were merely the money-getters and bridge builders of the world.

—*Ellis Meredith.*

April Fifth

Babies short and babies tall,
Babies big and babies small,
Blue-eyed babies, babies fair,
Brown-eyed babies with lots of hair.
Babies so tiny they can't sit up,
Babies that drink from a silver cup;
Babies that coo and babies that creep,
Babies that only can eat and sleep,
Babies that laugh and babies that talk,
Babies quite big enough to walk;
Dimpled fingers and dimpled feet,
What in the world is half so sweet
As babies that jump, laugh, cry and crawl,
Eat, sleep, talk, walk, creep, coo and all
Wee babies?

—*Eugene Field.*

April Sixth

A dreary place would be this earth,
  Were there no little people in it;
The song of life would lose its mirth,
  Were there no children to begin it.

No little forms, no buds to grow,
  And make the admiring heart surrender,
No little hands on breast and brow
  To keep the thrilling love-chords tender.

April Seventh

Look at me with thy large brown eyes,
      Philip, my king!
For 'round thee the purple shadow lies
  Of babyhood's royal dignities;
Lay on my neck thy tiny hand
  With love's invisible sceptre laden;
I am thine Esther, to command
  Till thou shall find thy queen handmaiden,
      Philip, my king!

—Dinah Muloch Craik.

April Eighth

The hope of the world lies in the fact that parents cannot make their children what they will.

—*W. E. Channing.*

Delight and liberty, the simple creed
Of childhood, whether busy or at rest.

—*William Wordsworth.*

April Ninth

"Art thou, weak Babe! my very God?
Oh, I must love Thee then,
Love Thee, and yearn to spread Thy love,
Among forgetful men.

"O sweet, O wakeful-hearted Child!
Sleep on, dear Jesus! sleep,
For Thou must one day wake for me
To suffer and to weep."

—*Frederick W. Faber.*

April Tenth

My mother sat in her room of nights now, after putting the babies to bed. I wonder if I might not have been a better woman if I had put my own children to bed and tucked them in and heard them say their prayers. I have heard mothers say the influence of that hour was as helpful to them as to the children.

—*Agnes Surbridge.*

April Eleventh

The earth, which feels the flowering of a thorn,
Was glad, O little child, when you were born;
The earth, which thrills when skylarks scale the blue,
Soared up itself to God's own heaven in you.

And heaven, which loves to lean down and to glass
Its beauty in each dewdrop on the grass,—
Heaven laughed to find your face so pure and fair,
And left, O little child, its reflex there!

William Canton.

April Twelfth

Strength and dignity are her clothing ;
And she laugheth at the time to come.
She openeth her mouth with wisdom ;
And the law of kindness is on her tongue.
She looketh well to the ways of her household,
And eateth not the bread of idleness ;
Her children rise up and call her blessed,
Her husband also and he praiseth her, saying,
  Many daughters have done virtuously,
  But thou excellest them all.

Proverbs 31 : 25–29.

April Thirteenth

" If thou appearest untouched by solemn thought,
  Thy nature is not therefore less divine.
Thou liest in Abraham's bosom all the year,
  And worshipest at the temple's inner shrine,
God being with thee when we know it not."

—William Wordsworth.

April Fourteenth

I found out long ago that those who get the best return from their flower gardens were those who kept no gardeners, and it is the same way with the child garden; those who are too over busy, irresponsible, ignorant, or rich to do without the orthodox nurse, never can know precisely what they lose. To watch a baby untrammelled with clothes, dimple, glow and expand in its bath, is in an intense degree like watching, early of a June morning, the first opening bud of a rose that you have coaxed and raised from a mere cutting. You hoped and believed that it would be fair and beautiful, but ah, what a glorious surprise it is!

(From "The People of the Whirlpool," by the author of "The Garden of a Commuter's Wife," copyrighted, 1903, by the Macmillan Company.)

April Fifteenth

So, one by one, the children have gone,
The boys were five and the girls were three;
And the big brown house is gloomy and lone,
With but two old folks for its company.
They talk to each other about the past,
As they sit together in eventide,
And say, "All the children we keep at last
Are the boys and the girl who in childhood died."

—*Anon.*

April Sixteenth

If you make children happy now, you will make them happy twenty years hence by the memory of it.

—*Sydney Smith.*

Who ran to help me when I fell,
And would some pretty story tell,
Or kiss the place to make it well?
My mother!

—*Jane Taylor.*

April Seventeenth

No time to pray!
Oh, who so fraught with earthly care
As not to give to humble prayer
Some part of day?

No time to pray!
Then sure your record falleth short;
Excuse will fail you as resort,
On that last day.

What thought more drear,
Than that our God His face should hide,
And say through all life's swelling tide,
No time to hear!

—*Anonymous.*

April Eighteenth

Ten children are loved by their parents where one child has his parents' sympathy. . . . Among those children who are not called to suffer from actual unkindness on the part of their parents, there is no greater cause of unhappiness than the lack of parental sympathy. . . . In his joys, as in his sorrows, a true child wants some one to share his feelings rather than to guide them.

—*H. Clay Trumbull.*

April Nineteenth

Last night, my darling, as you slept,
  I thought I heard you sigh ;
And to your little crib I crept,
  And watched a space thereby ;
And then I stooped and kissed your brow,
  For oh ! I love you so —
You are too young to know it now,
  But some time you shall know.

—*Eugene Field.*

April Twentieth

The children who have no toys, seize realities very late and never form ideals. . . . The nations rendered famous by their artists, artisans and idealists have supplied their infants with many toys, for there is more philosophy and poetry in a single doll than in a thousand books.

—*Seguin.*

April Twenty-first

Isn't it wonderful, when you think,
  How a little baby grows,
From his big, round eyes, that wink and blink,
  Down to his tiny toes?
Common thing is a baby, though,
  All play the baby's part,—
But all the whirling wheels that go,
Flying 'round while the ages flow,
  Can't make a baby's heart.

—*Julian S. Cutler.*

April Twenty-second

What would an engine be to a ship if it were lying loose in the hull? It must be fastened to it with bolts and screws before it can propel the vessel. Now, a childless man is like a loose engine. A man must be bolted and screwed to the community before he can work well for its advancement, and there are no such screws and bolts as children.

—*Henry Ward Beecher.*

April Twenty-third

Philosophy may boast of many a mind
Worthy the admiration of mankind;
A mind well stored with reasons and with laws,
To show the why, the wherefore, or the cause;
But in the highest realm of human thought,
The wise philosopher is wise for naught;
The child, in worship at his mother's knee,
May know and love a God as well as he.

—*Anon.*

April Twenty-fourth

Nothing, perhaps, has been more misunderstood than childhood.

—*James Sully.*

O dearest, dearest boy! My heart
For better lore would seldom yearn,
Could I but teach the hundredth part
Of what from thee I learn.

—*Anon.*

April Twenty-fifth

Hurrah for the little tin horse, the black, woolly dog, with the tiny red tongue! I shall never, perhaps, make their acquaintance, but their memory will ever be green and fragrant. They will go the way of the bossie cow who moo'ed and stayed out one night too late and lost her hide and "moo-er." But what would life be without the tin horse, the woolly dog, and the bossie cow that "moo-ed"?

—*H. W. Stough.*

April Twenty-sixth

And still, as the summer sunset
  Fades away in the west,
And the wee ones, tired of playing,
  Go trooping home to rest,
My husband calls from his corner,
  "Say, love, have the children come?"
And I answer, with eyes uplifted,
  "Yes, dear, they are all at home."

—*Margaret Sangster.*

April Twenty-seventh

Francis Xavier, the great Jesuit missionary, exhausted by days and nights of serving, said to his attendant, "I must sleep! I must sleep! If I do not, I shall die. If any one comes,—whoever comes, —waken me not. I must sleep!" He then retired to his tent, and his faithful servant began his watch. It was not long, however, till a pallid face appeared at the door. Xavier beckoned eagerly to the watcher and said in a solemn tone, "I made a mistake. I made a mistake. If a little child comes, waken me."

—*J. R. Miller.*

April Twenty-eighth

Lord, who ordainest for mankind
  Benignant toils and tender cares,
We thank Thee for the ties that bind
  The mother to the child she bears.
All-Gracious! grant to those that bear
  A mother's charge, the strength and light
To lead the steps that own their care
  In ways of love and truth and light.

—*William Cullen Bryant.*

April Twenty-ninth

Let parents then bequeath to their children, not riches, but the spirit of reverence.

—*Plato.*

Youth fades; love droops; the leaves of friendship
fall;
A mother's secret hope outlives them all!

—*Oliver Wendell Holmes.*

April Thirtieth

The sweetest sound heard through our earthly home,
The brightest ray that gleams from heaven's dome,
The loveliest flower that e'er from earth's breast rose,
That purest flame that, quivering, gleams and glows,
Are found alone, where kneels a mother mild,
With heart uplifted, praying for her child.

—*Anonymous.*

The Month of May

May First

A little figure glided through the hall.
  "Is that you, Pet?" the word came tenderly.
A sob, suppressed to let the answer fall,—
  "It isn't Pet, mamma, it's only me!"

The quivering baby lips! They had not meant
  To utter any word could plant a sting,
But to that mother-heart a strange pang went,
  She heard, and stood like a convicted thing.

One instant, and the happy little face
  Thrilled 'neath unwonted kisses rained above;
And from that moment "Only Me" had place
  And part with Pet in tender mother-love.

—Caroline A. Mason.

May Second

Blessed be the hand that prepares a pleasure for a child, for there is no saying when and where it will blossom forth.

—Douglas Jerrold.

God bless the men and women of noble brain and
  heart,
Who go down in the folk-swamps and take the children's part.

—Will Carleton.

May Third

The wise mother, training her daughter not for the moment but for all time, will realize that there are no small things where a child is concerned; that some things, apparently the most trivial, will have far-reaching results, and therefore with a critical eye she will scan all influences that surround the infant and eliminate all that seem in the least calculated to interfere with her most harmonious development.

—*Mary Wood-Allen.*

May Fourth

Let the history of your domestic rule typify, in little, the history of our political rule; at the outset, autocratic control, where control is really needful; by and by an incipient constitutionalism, in which the liberty of the subject gains some express recognition; successive extensions of this liberty of the subject; gradually ending in parental abdication.

—*Herbert Spencer.*

May Fifth

It is not right to wish for death; the Lord disposes best.
His Spirit comes to quiet hearts and fits them for His rest;
And that He halved our little flock was merciful, I see,
For Benjamin has two in heaven,—and two are left with me.

—*Bayard Taylor.*

May Sixth

"I'm not a baby," growled Donald, savagely. "I'm not a baby any more; I'm a boy."

And the childish lips that trembled babyishly even while they made stalwart assertion, spoke the truth. For doubt and unbelief have no place in a baby's world, and Donald's eyes were looking dimly into a universe of shaken trust, of broken faith. He knew well enough that there was no Santa Claus, but it was not for the pudgy old saint that he grieved. It was for the lost trust in his mother, the confidence destroyed.

—*Kathryn Jarboe.*

May Seventh

You used to long for some definite proof of God. All thoughtful men long for that. And I have found the best living parable in the Pearl. You know what her mother is to her. She is as God to her. I believe in God now, because I believe in a mother. When I see the daily miracle of motherhood, it would be unthinkable to me if you and I had no such daily motherhood in the Eternal. We could do just as well without God as the Rogue could do without her mother. A man would have as little meaning without a God as a child without a mother. You will find it useless to *argue* with a sceptic about God—arguments help so little—and you cannot demonstrate the Unseen in black and white. But before a man says there is no God, ask him if he can explain away the miracle of a mother. He will not be able to do it, for he cannot explain away himself. And when you have got him to realize the miracle of motherhood he will not be very far from believing in a God. Do not *hurry* his faith after that, but wait until he has a child of his own. Then he will find it as easy to believe as it was once easy to doubt. This may be nursery theology, but I expect it is good enough for you and me.

—From "The Finest Baby in the World"
by "Theadorer."

May Eighth

A place for the boys, dear mother, I pray,
As cares settle down round our short earthly way;
Don't let us forget, by our kind, loving deeds,
To show we remember their pleasures and needs,
Though our souls may be vexed with problems of life,
And worn with besetments and toilings and strife,
Our hearts will keep younger,—your tired heart and mine —
If we give them a place in their innermost shrine;
And to our life's latest hour 'twill be one of our joys
That we kept a small corner,—a place for the boys.

—*Boston Transcript.*

May Ninth

A mother who turns her children over to the care of others,—who knows not what it is to labour with them and for them in the minute details of their spiritual and bodily lives, cannot feel the loss of them as keenly as the mother who is unhappy if they are not close to her night and day, for "love grows by serving."

—*Patterson Du Bois.*

May Tenth

To you is the promise, and to your children.

—*Acts 2 : 39.*

Does the Parent of all of us resign His authority when He humors us in *our* childish ways, because we can't comprehend any greater ones? Every concession is followed by growth on the part of His children, if they are honest; when they're not, it seems to me the concessions aren't made. But my children are honest.

—*John Habberton.*

May Eleventh

How will they build, these little hands?
Upon the treacherous, shifting sands,
Or where the rock eternal stands?
And will they fashion strong and true
The work that they shall find to do?
Dear little hands, if I but knew!
Could I but see the veilèd fate
Behind your barred and hidden gate!

—*Anon.*

May Twelfth

I know that a sweet child is the sweetest thing in nature, not even excepting the delicate creatures which bear them; but the prettier the kind of a thing is, the more desirable it is that it should be pretty of its kind.

One daisy differs not much from another in glory, but a violet should look and smell the daintiest.

—Charles Lamb.

May Thirteenth

Greatest of crimes is the hurting of a child's soul.

—J. R. Miller.

It seems impossible they should ever grow to be men, and drag the heavy artillery along the dusty roads of life.

—H. W. Longfellow.

A torn jacket is soon mended; but hard words bruise the heart of a child.

—H. W. Longfellow.

May Fourteenth

Sleep, baby, sleep;
Your father tends the sheep;
Your mother shakes the branches small,
Whence happy dreams in showers fall;
Sleep, baby, sleep.

Sleep, baby, sleep;
The sky is full of sheep;
The stars the lambs of heaven are,
For whom the Shepherd moon doth care;
Sleep, baby, sleep.

Sleep, baby, sleep;
The Christ Child owns the sheep
He is Himself the Lamb of God,
The world to save, to death He trod;
Sleep, baby, sleep.

—*German Cradle Song.*

May Fifteenth

It is one of the hardest yet most necessary duties of a woman's life to carry on with attention, harmony, and serenity the several parallel threads of her household life; every one demands her constant care, the relation between every one must be kept, and she must be strong enough to fulfill hourly, even momentarily, claims upon her intellect, heart and patience.

—*Mrs. Frank Malleson.*

May Sixteenth

"What see I now?
The lamps are lit, the fires burn bright,
The house is filled with life and light,
It is the Golden Wedding Day!
The tramping children crowd the stair,
And in and out and everywhere
Flashes along the corridor
The sunshine of their golden hair.
The ancient bridegroom and the bride
Behold, well pleased, on every side
Their forms and features multiplied."

—*Anon.*

May Seventeenth

One blessed thing about Ian,—even though he is sometimes passionate and stubborn and will probably have lots of trouble with himself by and by,—there isn't a drop of sneaky blood in him, which is the only trait that need make a mother tremble.

(From "The People of the Whirlpool," by the author of "The Garden of a Commuter's Wife," copyrighted, 1903, by the Macmillan Company.)

May Eighteenth

All that is purest and best in man is but the echo of a mother's benediction. The hero's deeds are a mother's prayers fulfilled.

—*Frederick W. Morton.*

O'erweening mother-love, that still can see
In furrowed brow and bearded lips, the trace
Of that she holds most dear in memory,
Love's dimpled prototype,—a baby's face.

—*Marion F. Ham.*

May Nineteenth

There is an exquisite poetry in the spontaneous promptings of the unsophisticated spirit of the child. So far removed at times from our one-sided prejudiced views, so high above our low conventional standards, are the little one's intuitions of his new world.

—*James Sully.*

May Twentieth

If I could lay my hand upon the heart
  That moulders underneath the church-yard snows,
And bid the sleeping pulses wake and start,
  And to the faded lips restore the rose;

If I could lead the precious child you love,
  With shrinking footsteps to his earthly place;
If I could bring him from the fold above,
  The tangled paths of life again to trace;

Say! would you bid him lay his glory by,
  That you might hold him to your troubled breast?
And would your yearning mother-heart deny
  The good to him, that you might thus be blest?

—*Mary Riley Smith.*

May Twenty-first

For this child I prayed; and the Lord hath given me my petition which I asked of Him: therefore I also have granted him to the Lord; as long as he liveth he is granted to the Lord.

(Hannah's prayer for Samuel.—1 Samuel 1: 27, 28.)

You must not expect that lives lived apart for so many years can be made alike all at once. We would not have it so; but the very process of harmonizing,—when the Christ spirit guides it, the little obstacles overcome,—the little surrenders of individuality made,—are no less wonderful. A woman's greatest joy is her complete surrender to her husband. A man doesn't understand all that it means to a woman, he cannot; and the very fact that he does not makes the surrender more complete, the gift more holy.

—*Helen Russ Stough.*

May Twenty-second

My idea of a boy; he is half angel and half animal. He is wideawake all night camping out, but falls asleep in church. He is superstitious, giving a dandelion three puffs to see if his mother wants him. He carries a lucky stone in his pocket. He cures warts by burying a dish-rag. Burnt cork, feathers, pins, father's barn, make a whole day's show. He stones the dogs, but will work for hours over a dog that limps with a broken leg to the back door. No kinder heart ever cared for a motherless lamb. He disturbs family worship, but who makes us think more of heaven when he kneels and prays? He is half angel and half animal.

—*Sydney Strong.*

May Twenty-third

Mother is the name for God in the lips and hearts of little children.

—*William M. Thackeray.*

When God thought of MOTHER, He must have laughed with satisfaction and framed it quickly,—so rich, so deep, so divine, so full of soul, power and beauty was the conception.

—*Henry Ward Beecher.*

May Twenty-fourth

Just as a mother, with sweet, pious face,
  Yearns towards her little children from her seat,
Gives one a kiss, another an embrace,
  Takes this upon her knees, that on her feet;
And while from actions, looks, complaints, pretenses,
  She learns their feelings and their various will,
To this a look, to that a word dispenses,
  And, whether stern or smiling, loves them still,—
So Providence for us, high, infinite,
  Makes our necessities its watchful task,
Hearkens to all our prayers, helps all our wants,
And e'en if it denies what seems our right,
  Either denies because 'twould have us ask,
Or seems but to deny, and in denying grants.

—*Filicaja, translated by Leigh Hunt.*

May Twenty-fifth

To what genius fed on tears shall we some day owe that most touching of elegies,—the tale of tortures borne silently by souls whose tender roots find stony ground in the domestic soil, whose earliest buds are torn apart by rancorous hands, whose flowers are touched by frost at the moment of their blossoming?

—*Balzac.*

May Twenty-sixth

I regard marriage as a partnership, in which each partner is in honour bound to think of the rights of the other as well as of his or her own. But I think that the duties are even more important than the rights, and in the long run I think that the reward is ampler and greater for duty well done than for the insistence upon individual rights, necessary though this, too, must often be. Your duty is hard, your responsibility great; but greatest of all is your reward. I do not pity you in the least. On the contrary, I feel respect and admiration for you.

—*Theodore Roosevelt.*

May Twenty-seventh

Teaching a child to do right is in itself teaching it not to do wrong.

—*Ennes Richmond.*

There is no shirking it; as we train our children, so are we responsible for the welfare of the world of the future; we cannot leave them alone, they cannot stand still, they must go backwards or forwards, and on us, on us alone, depends the result.

—*Ennes Richmond.*

May Twenty-eighth

Just a little baby lying in my arms,
Would that I could keep you with your baby charms;
Helpless, clinging fingers; downy, golden hair,
Where the sunshine lingers, caught from otherwhere;
Roly-poly shoulders, dimple in your cheek;
Dainty little blossom, in a world of woe;
Thus I fain would keep you, for I love you so.

—*Louise C. Moulton.*

May Twenty-ninth

Wherever a true wife comes, home is always round her. The stars only may be over her head, the glow-worm in the night-cold grass may be the only fire at her foot, but home is yet wherever she is.

—*John Ruskin.*

Maids must be wives and mothers, to fulfill
Th' entire and holiest woman's being.

—*Frances Anne Kemble.*

May Thirtieth

"Who was the greatest man that ever lived, grandfather?"

"Jesus of Nazareth, boy."

"And who was the greatest soldier?"

"Ulysses S. Grant."

"And the next greatest?"

"George Washington."

"Who was the greatest woman that ever lived, grandfather?"

"Your mother, boy."

"Oh, father," it was mother's voice, "you forget."

"Forget nothing," cried grandfather, fiercely. "Boy, your mother is the best woman that ever lived, and mind you remember it, too. Every boy's mother is the best woman that ever lived."

—*Roy Rolfe Gilson.*

⚜

May Thirty-first

My child, my glorious, translated child!
From the deep beauty of thine angel home
Would I, in yearnings vain, or wishes wild,
Withdraw thy feet, o'er earth's rough ways to roam,—
Wither the rose upon thy brow that lies,
And dim the light of heaven from thy dear eyes?
No! to my love for thee let power be given
To draw, not thee to earth, but me to heaven.

—*Mae Myrtle.*

The Month of

June First

No ordinary work done by a man is either as hard or as responsible as the work of a woman who is bringing up a family of small children; for upon her time and strength demands are made not only every hour of the day but often every hour of the night. She may have to get up night after night to take care of a sick child, and yet must by day continue to do all her household duties as well, and if the family means are scant, she must usually enjoy even her rare holidays taking her whole brood of children with her. The birth pangs make all men the debtors of all women.

—*Theodore Roosevelt.*

June Second

A mother's prayers, silent and gentle, can never miss the road to the throne of all bounty.

—*Henry Ward Beecher.*

And if God wills that even baby feet
  Shall feel the sharpness of life's toilsome way,
Be sure that recompense most full and sweet
  Is waiting for these little ones some day.

—*Mary Riley Smith.*

June Third

How should we like to live, half of the time, in a place where the piano was twelve feet tall, the door knobs at an impossible height, and the mantel shelf in the sky; where every mortal thing was out of reach except a collection of highly interesting objects on dressing-tables and bureaus, guarded however, by giants and giantesses, three times as large and powerful as ourselves, forever saying, "mustn't touch"; and if we did touch we should be spanked, and have no other method of revenge save to spank back symbolically on the inoffensive persons of our dolls?

—*Kate Douglas Wiggin.*

June Fourth

The most important part of education is right training in the nursery.

—*Plato.*

It is the hour when children's prayers,
Like perfume from the lilies rise;
When all the angels cry, "Oh, list!"
And God makes silence in the skies.

—*Mary Riley Smith.*

June Fifth

She is now a woman of thirty-six, in the full glow of her matronly beauty, in perfect health because she was wise enough not to violate nature's laws; as brimful of life and the joy of living as she was at eighteen; filled with happiness and gladness and shedding both upon those she loves, holding their love and respect by right of her womanliness, her dignity, her tenderness; guiding and guarding her children; their queen because they have weighed her in their childish scales of justice, which are, oh, so true, and have not found one scruple wanting.

—*Gabrielle E. Jackson.*

June Sixth

The childhood shows the man as morning shows the day.

—*John Milton.*

The love principle is stronger than the force principle.

—*A. A. Hodge.*

The best way of training the young is to train yourself at the same time; not to admonish them but to be always carrying out your own principles in practice.

—*Plato.*

June Seventh

Thou art come to Thy beautiful Mother;
She hath looked on Thy marvellous face;
Thou art come to us, Maker of Mary!
And she was Thy channel of grace.

Thou hast brought with Thee plentiful pardon,
And our souls overflow with delight;
Our hearts are half broken, dear Jesus!
With the joy of this wonderful night.

—*Frederick W. Faber.*

June Eighth

There is a world of childhood, underrated, misunderstood, slighted, snubbed, thwarted, oppressed. Yet while the children whom our Lord thought worthy of exalting as our model, are held in the meanest kind of subjection by those who love them they remain bravely patient and loyal.

—*Patterson Du Bois.*

June Ninth

But, never, in her varied sphere,
Is woman to the heart more dear
Than when her homely task she plies,
With cheerful duty in her eyes;
And, every lowly path well trod,
Looks meekly upward to her God.

—*Caroline Gilman.*

June Tenth

Still slip on the years, like brimming bowls of nectar. Another Madge is sister to Frank, and a little Nelly is younger sister to this other Madge.

Three of them—a charmed and mystic number,—which if it be broken in these young days, as alas, it may be! will only yield a cherub angel to float over you, and to float over them,—to wean you and to wean them from this world, where all joys do perish, to that seraph world where joys do last forever.

—*Donald G. Mitchell.*

June Eleventh

His startled eyes with wonder see
A father near him, on his knee,
Who wishes all the while to trace
The mother in his future face;
But 'tis to her, alone, uprise
His wakening arms: to her those eyes
Open with joy and not surprise.

—*Walter Savage Landor.*

June Twelfth

You have no children, Kavanagh; we have five.

Ah, so many already! A living Pentateuch! A beautiful Pentapylon or five-gated temple of Life!

—*H. W. Longfellow.*

There is something exceeding thrilling in the voices of children singing.

—*H. W. Longfellow.*

June Thirteenth

Prince thou art,—the grown up man
Only is republican.
Let the million-dollared ride!
Barefoot, trudging at his side,
Thou hast more than he can buy
In the reach of ear and eye,—
Outward sunshine, inward joy;
Blessings on thee, barefoot boy!

—*John G. Whittier.*

June Fourteenth

This child is greater than any man in Greece; for the Athenians command the Greeks, I command the Athenians, his mother commands me, and he commands his mother.

—*Themistocles.*

Hereditary rank may be a snare and a delusion, but hereditary virtue is a patent of innate nobility which far outshines the blazonry of heraldry.

—*Washington Irving.*

June Fifteenth

Where did you come from, baby dear?
Out of the everywhere into here.

Where did you get your eyes so blue?
Out of the sky as I came through.

Where did you get this pearly ear?
God spoke, and it came out to hear.

Where did you get that little tear?
I found it waiting when I got here.

But how did you come to us, you dear?
God thought of you, and so I am here.

—*George MacDonald.*

June Sixteenth

To be a mother is the grandest vocation in the world. No being has a position of such power and influence. She holds in her hands the destiny of nations; for to her is necessarily committed the making of the nation's citizens.

—*Hannah Whitall Smith.*

In the man whose childhood has known caresses there lies a fibre of memory which can be touched to noble issues.

—*George Eliot.*

June Seventeenth

And home will sweeten in the coming days,
When widening love shall warm these human ways;
When every mother, pressing to her face,
Her child, shall clasp all children of the race.
Then will the rafter and the oaken beam
Be laid in music and the poet's dream —
Then Earth, as far as flies the feathered foam,
Shall have in it the friendly feel of home.

—*Edwin Markham.*

June Eighteenth

All education to beauty, is, first, in the beauty of gentle human faces round a child; secondly, in the fields, fields meaning grass, water, beasts, flowers, sky, without these no man can be educated humanly. If a child has other things right around it, and given to it its garden, its cat and its window to the skies and stars—in time pictures of flowers, and beasts, and things, in heaven and heavenly earth, may be useful to it. But see first that its realities are heavenly.

—*John Ruskin.*

June Nineteenth

O little feet! that such long years
Must wander on through hopes and fears,
Must ache and bleed beneath your load;
I, nearer to the wayside inn
Where toil shall cease and rest begin,
Am weary thinking of your road!

—*Henry Wadsworth Longfellow.*

For the noblest man that lives there still remains a conflict.

—*James A. Garfield.*

June Twentieth

Backward, turn backward, O time, in your flight,
Make me a child again, just for to-night!
Mother, come back from the echoless shore,
Take me again to your heart as of yore;
Kiss from my forehead the furrows of care,
Smooth the few silver threads out of my hair;
Over my slumbers your loving watch keep;
Rock me to sleep, mother, rock me to sleep!

—*Elizabeth Akers Allen.*

June Twenty-first

Train up a child in the way he should go and even when he is old he will not depart from it.

—*Proverbs 22 : 6.*

Children rarely love those who spoil them, and never trust them. Their keen young sense detects the false note in the character and draws its own conclusions, which are generally very just.

—*Selected.*

June Twenty-second

Long, long before the babe could speak,
When he would kiss his mother's cheek,
  And to her bosom press,
The brightest angels, standing near,
Would turn away to hide a tear,
  For they are motherless.

—*J. B. Tabb.*

June Twenty-third

Said a mother to me one day: "When my children were young I thought the very best thing I could do for them was to give them myself. So I spared no pains to talk with them, to teach them, to pray with them, to be a loving companion and friend to my children. I had to neglect my house often. I had no time to indulge myself in many things which I should have liked to do. I was so busy adorning their minds and cultivating their hearts' best affections that I could not adorn their bodies in fine clothes, though I kept them neat and comfortable at all times.

"I have my reward now. I have a thousand beautiful memories of their childhood to comfort me. Now that they have gone out into the world, I have the sweet consciousness of having done all I could to make them ready for whatever work God calls them to do."

—*Selected.*

June Twenty-fourth

Baby and I with the morning gray,
Are griping and squalling and walking away;
The fire's gone out and I nearly freeze;
There's a smell of peppermint on the breeze;
Then mama wakes
And baby takes
And says, "Now cook the breakfast, please!"

—*Eugene Field.*

June Twenty-fifth

Better be driven out from among men, than to be disliked of children.

—*Dana.*

"Beware," said Lavater, "of him who hates the laugh of a child."

"I love God and little children," was the simple yet sublime sentiment of Richter.

—*Lydia H. Sigourney.*

June Twenty-sixth

Nor will I burden my days with sighs,
  Lest God for my child should send;
For whether he lives, or whether he dies,
  He is mine till eternity's end.
And I fear no harm to baby or me
  Since both, O! Father, belong to Thee!

—*Mary Riley Smith.*

June Twenty-seventh

Not pain, not temper, but the unconscious yearning for companionship, for mother-love, is oftener the motive of the pitiful cry. Why should it be denied? The mother bird broods her young in the nest at twilight, and the father bird sings a lullaby to both. The kittens luxuriously sup themselves to sleep with the warm mother flesh responding to their seeking paws. In wild life I know of not an animal who does not in some way soothe her young to sleep. Why should the human child, the son of man, be forced to live without the dream memories that linger about the happy sleeping times? What can the vaunted discipline give to replace them?

(From "The People of the Whirlpool," by the author of "The Garden of a Commuter's Wife," copyrighted, 1903, by the Macmillan Company.)

June Twenty-eighth

Sleep, babe, the honeyed sleep of innocence!
  Sleep like a bud, for soon the sun of life
With ardours quick and passionate shall rise,
  And, with half kisses, part thy fragrant life—
    The folded petals of thy soul.

—*J. G. Holland.*

(From "Bittersweet," published by Charles Scribner's Sons.)

June Twenty-ninth

Nothing can compare in beauty, and wonder, and admirableness, and divinity itself, to the silent work in obscure dwellings of faithful women bringing their children to honour and virtue and piety.

I tell you the inside is larger than the outside: for the loom is more than the fabric; the thinker more than the thought; the builder more than the building.

—*H. W. Beecher.*

June Thirtieth

The lesson of choosing the good,—this is the lesson of all lessons for us to begin to inculcate in our little children. —*Ennes Richmond.*

O wondrous power! How little understood!
Entrusted to the mother's mind alone,
To fashion genius, form the soul for good.
—*Sarah J. Hale.*

The Month of July

July First

Like a cradle rocking, rocking,
  Silent, peaceful, to and fro;
Like a mother's sweet looks dropping
  On the little face below,
Hangs the green earth, swinging, turning,
  Jarless, noiseless, safe and slow;
Falls the light of God's face bending
  Down and watching us below.
And as feeble babes that suffer,
  Toss and cry, and will not rest,
Are the ones the tender mother
  Holds the closest, loves the best:
So, when we are weak and wretched,
  By our sins weighed down, distressed,
Then it is that God's great patience
  Holds us closest, loves us best.

—*Saxe Holm.*

July Second

Home is the sacred refuge of our life.

—Dryden.

Every child's birthright is a happy home. No human foresight can provide for the child a happy life. The future may be full of shoals and quicksands. But there is gladness enough to go round the whole world while the children are little and in the home nest.

—Margaret Sangster.

July Third

Nae shoon to hide her tiny taes,
  Nae stockings on her feet,
Her supple ankles white as snaw,
  Or early blossoms sweet.

Her simple dress of sprinkled pink,
  Her double, dimpled chin,
Her puckered lip and baumy mou'
  With nae ane tooth between.

Her een sae like her mither's een,
  Twa gentle, liquid things;
Her face is like an angel's face—
  We're glad she has nae wings!

Hugh Miller.

July Fourth

I think the tendency is to exalt maternity at the expense of paternity, to make the mother everything and the father incidental. I don't believe in that, not one bit, and I think it accounts for the large number of badly trained children.

—*Ellis Meredith.*

July Fifth

How should I love the pretty creatures
  While 'round my knees they fondly clung,
To see them look their mother's features,
  To hear them lisp their mother's tongue!

And when with envy, Time, transported,
  Shall think to rob us of our joys,
You'll in your girls again be courted,
  And I'll go wooing in my boys.

—*Anon.*

July Sixth

But one thing upon earth is better than the wife, —that is the mother.

—*Leopold Shefer.*

A man takes counsel with his wife, he obeys his mother: he obeys her long after she has ceased to live: and the ideas which he has received from her become principles stronger even than his passions.

—*Aimi Martin.*

July Seventh

Children are what the mothers are,
No fondest father's fondest care
Can fashion so the infant heart
As those creative beams that dart,
With all their hopes and fears, upon
The cradle of a sleeping son.

—*Walter Savage Landor.*

July Eighth

Parents! A child is naturally trustful; guide its young trust to that Word which never fails.

—*Andrew Murray.*

Lo, children are an heritage of the Lord:
And the fruit of the womb is His reward.
As arrows are in the hand of a mighty man;
So are children of the youth.
Happy is the man that hath his quiver full of them.

—*Psalm 127: 3–5.*

July Ninth

Children grow up so quickly and leave us, and I would long that mine should take nothing but the recollection of love and happiness from their home with them into the world's fight, knowing that they have here always a safe harbor and open arms to comfort and encourage them when they are in trouble.

—*Princess Alice, Grand Duchess.*

July Tenth

"Mama, is there too many of we?"
The little girl asked with a sigh,
"Perhaps you wouldn't be tired, you see
If a few of your childs should die."
There were half a dozen round her stood,
And the mother was sick and poor,
Worn out with the care of the noisy brood,
And the fight with the wolf at the door.

Only a week, and the little Clare
In her tiny white trundle-bed,
Lay with blue eyes closed, and the shining hair
Cut close to the golden head.
"Don't cry," she said,—and the words were low,
Feeling tears that she could not see,—
"You won't have to work and be tired so,
When there ain't so many of we."

—*Anon.*

July Eleventh

My children! My children! they clustered all round me,
Like a rampart which sorrow could never break through;
Each change in their beautiful lives only bound me
In a spell of delight which no care could undo.

—*Frederick W. Faber.*

July Twelfth

He who helps a child helps humanity with a distinctness, with an immediateness which no other help given to human creatures at any other stage of their human life, can possibly give again.

—*Phillips Brooks.*

The greatest and wisest have not only worked for the children, but have learned from the children.

—*Sydney Strong.*

July Thirteenth

Do ye hear the children weeping, oh, my brothers,
  E'er the sorrow comes with years?
They are leaning their young heads against their
    mothers,
  And that cannot stop their tears.
The young lambs are bleating in the meadows,
  The young birds are chirping in the nest,
The young fawns are playing with the shadows,
  The young flowers are blowing towards the west—
But the young, young children, O My brothers,
  They are weeping bitterly!
They are weeping in the playtime of the others,
  In the country of the free.

—*Elizabeth Barrett Browning.*

July Fourteenth

In a single day, I, a strong man with nothing else to occupy my mind, am reduced to physical and mental worthlessness by the necessities of two boys not over mischievous or bad. And you—heaven only knows how—have unbroken weeks, months, years, yes, lifetimes of just such experiences, and with them the burden of household cares, of physical ills, and depressions, of mental anxieties that pierce your hearts with as many sorrows as grieved the Holy Mother of old.

—*John Habberton.*

July Fifteenth

I wonder so that mothers ever fret
At little children clinging to their gown;
Or that the footprints, when the days are wet,
Are ever black enough to make them frown.
If I could find a little muddy boot,
Or cap or jacket, on my chamber floor;
If I could kiss a rosy, restless foot,
And hear it patter in my home once more!

—*Mary Riley Smith.*

July Sixteenth

When Antipater demanded fifty children as hostages from the Spartans, they offered him, in their stead, a hundred men of distinction, unlike ordinary educators, who precisely reverse the offering. The Spartans thought rightly and nobly. In the world of childhood all posterity stands before us upon which we, like Moses upon the promised land, may only gaze but not enter; and at the same time, it renews for us the ages of the young world behind which we must appear.

—*Jean Paul Richter.*

July Seventeenth

Nor ends when cruel death lays low
  In dust each little curly head,
All sovereigns crownless go,
  And are forgotten, when they're dead.

But these hold changeless empire past,
  Triumphant past, all earthly scenes;
We worship, truest to the last,
  The buried little kings and queens.

—*Helen Hunt.*

July Eighteenth

When our infancy is almost forgotten, and our boyhood long departed though it seems but as yesterday; when life settles darkly down upon us, and we doubt whether to call ourselves young any more, then it is good to steal away from the society of bearded men, and even of gentle women, and spend an hour or two with children. After drinking from those fountains of still fresh existence, we shall return into the crowd to struggle onward and do our part in life, perhaps as fervently as ever, but, for a time, with a kinder and purer heart, and a spirit more lightly wise.

—*Nathaniel Hawthorne.*

July Nineteenth

Thou'st seen how closely, Abba, when at rest
My child's head nestles to my breast,
And how my arm her little form enfolds,
Lest in the darkness she should feel alone;
And how she holds
My hands, my hands, my two hands in her own?
A little easeful sighing
And restful turning round,
And I too, on Thy love relying,
Shall slumber sound.

—*William Canton.*

July Twentieth

And these words which I command thee this day, shall be in thine heart. And thou shalt teach them diligently unto thy children, and shalt talk of them when thou sittest in thine house, and when thou walkest by the way, and when thou liest down, and when thou risest up.

—*Deuteronomy* 6 : 6, 7.

The voices that spoke to me when a child, are now speaking through me to the world.

—*Bishop A. B. Simpson.*

July Twenty-first

How many miles to Baby-land?
Any one can tell,
Up one flight,
To your right,
Please to ring the bell.

What can you see in Baby-land?
Little folks in white;
Downy heads,
Cradle beds,
Faces pure and bright.

—*Eugene Field.*

July Twenty-second

As life wears on, the love of husband or wife, of friends and of children, becomes the great solace and delight of age. The one recalls the past, the other gives interest to the future; and in our children, it has been truly said, we live our lives again.

—Sir John Lubbock.

July Twenty-third

I am to have a child. Flesh of my flesh,
Soul of my soul, and love of earthly love!
In marvel of thanksgiving do I kneel
To pledge that coming life to God above.

The throbbing of my pulse shall live anew;
Where I have stumbled she shall firmly tread;
Where sin has dimmed my vision she shall see;
Of my night's darkness she shall know no dread.

In valleys my path led, but when I bear
My Baby-one aloft no sight shall mar
Her view beyond the hills where beauties lie
That I see now, because I came afar.

Wonder of wonders! Life that gives increase,
Spring to the winter and a child to me!
Within the Future's pool I see a face
Like to my own—as God would have it be.

—Edith Livingston Smith.

July Twenty-fourth

What we no longer possess—the all quickening, creative power of child-life—let it again be translated from their life into ours. . . . Let us live for our children: then will the life of our children bring us peace and joy; then shall we begin to grow wise, to be wise.

—*Froebel.*

July Twenty-fifth

The baby wept,
The mother took it from the nurse's arms,
And soothed its griefs, and stilled its vain alarms,
And baby slept.

Again it weeps,
And God doth take it from mother's arms,
From present pain and future unknown harms,
And baby sleeps.

—*Samuel Hinds.*

July Twenty-sixth

Home indeed may be a sure haven of repose from the storms and perils of the world. But to secure this we must not be content to pave it with good intentions, but must make it bright and cheerful.

If our life be one of toil and of suffering, if the world outside be cold and dreary, what a pleasure to return to the sunshine of happy faces and the warmth of hearts we love.

—*Sir John Lubbock.*

July Twenty-seventh

As for me and my house, we will serve the Lord.

—*Joshua 24: 15.*

Oh, that the ruling principle of parental life and love, might be,—without this child I will not see my Father's face.

—*Andrew Murray.*

July Twenty-eighth

There are physical mothers and there are spiritual mothers, and there are those who combine the two. It is a mistaken idea, to suppose that because a woman has given birth to a child this fact makes her a mother in the highest sense of the word.

I could show you women who have given birth to five or six, even ten, children without possessing, apparently, a single spark of real motherhood.

—Elizabeth Harrison.

July Twenty-ninth

Grant us, O Lord, the grace to bear
  The little pricking thorn ;
The hasty word that seems unsaid ;
  The twang of truth well worn ;
The jest which makes our weakness plain ;
  The darling plan o'erturned ;
The careless touch upon our pain ;
  The slight we have not earned.
The rasp of care, dear Lord, to-day
  Lest all these fretting things
Make needless grief, oh, give, we pray,
  The heart that trusts and sings.

—Elizabeth L. Gould.

July Thirtieth

What a happy hour it is, this one of story telling, dear and sacred to every child-lover! What an eager, delightful audience are these little ones, grieving at the sorrows of the heroes, laughing at their successes, breathless with anxiety lest the cat catch the disobedient mouse, clapping hands when the Ugly Duckling is changed into the Swan, all appreciation, all interest, all joy! We might count the rest of the world well lost, could we ever be surrounded by such blooming faces, such loving hearts, and such ready sympathy.

—*Kate D. Wiggin.*

July Thirty-first

A little dreaming, such as mothers know;
  A little lingering over dainty things;
A happy heart, wherein hope all aglow
  Stirs like a bird at dawn that wakes and sings,
          And that is all.

A little clasping to her yearning breast;
  A little musing over future years;
A heart that prays: "Dear Lord, Thou knowest best—
  But spare my flower life's bitterest rain of tears"—
          And that is all.

—*Macmillan's Magazine.*

The Month of

August First

Retzsch, a German sculptor, made a wonderful statue of the Redeemer. For eight years it was his dream by night and his thought by day. He first made a clay model, and set it before a child five or six years old. There were about the figure none of the usual emblematical marks designating the Saviour —no cross, no crown of thorns, by which to identify it. Yet when the child saw it, and was asked who it was, he said, " Suffer little children and forbid them not to come unto Me."

—J. R. Miller.

August Second

With babes that in their cradles sleep,
Or cling to you in perfect trust,
Think of the mothers left to weep
Their infants lying in the dust.

And when the step you wait for comes,
And all your world is full of light,
O woman safe in happy homes,
Pray for all lonesome souls to-night!

—Anon.

August Third

Every fault is, simply, the lack of some virtue. If that virtue is cultivated and developed, the fault will die for want of nourishment. Let the mother try then to make her children in love with goodness, and WIN them to it, instead of DRIVING them, she will accomplish far more for their characters than by any amount of what is called "strict discipline."

—*Hannah Whitall Smith.*

August Fourth

The green tendrils of the growing vine must wind 'round something.

—*O. W. Holmes.*

A boy's will is the wind's will,
And the thoughts of youth are long, long thoughts.

—*H. W. Longfellow.*

August Fifth

Thou atom of the ages,
  Thou force among the forces
  Out from the Source of sources,
Thou puzzler of the sages,
Back comes to me thy mimicry;
This heart of mine beats on in thine,
    One life Divine —
      Thy destiny
        In me.

—Patterson Du Bois.

August Sixth

If you are setting up false lights for them, when you come to gather up the wreckage and booty of your lives, washed upon the eternal shores, your dim, lurid lights will reveal to you the upturned faces of your own children—lost! Oh, beware how you lead one of God's little ones astray!

—J. R. Miller.

But whoso shall offend one of these little ones which believe in Me, it were better for him that a millstone were hanged about his neck, and that he were drowned in the depth of the sea.

—Matthew 18: 6.

August Seventh

Praying for the little people
  (Closed are eyes of brown and blue),
By the quiet bedside kneeling
With a trustful, sure appealing;
All the Spirit's guidance needing,
Seeking it with earnest pleading—
  This is what the mothers do.

Parting from the little people.
  (Heart of mine how fast they grow!)
Fashioning the wedding dresses,
Treasuring the last caresses;
Waiting then as years fly faster
For the summons of the Master—
  This is what the mothers do.

—*Mary L. C. Robinson.*

August Eighth

In old times there used to be a strong place in every castle, called the keep. It was the place where all the weak and helpless and precious things were hidden in times of danger. God is our Keep, and we must hide in His safe care and keeping our precious children. If we are hidden in this Divine Keep ourselves, surely we will not leave our children outside.

—*Hannah Whitall Smith.*

August Ninth

No babe within our arms to leap,
  No little eyes towards slumber tending;
No little knees in prayer to bend,
  Our lips the sweet words lending.

The sterner souls would get more stern,
  Unfeeling natures more inhuman,
And man in stoic coldness turn,
  And woman would be less than woman.

—*Anon.*

August Tenth

My righteousness shall be forever, and my salvation from generation to generation.

—*Isaiah 51 : 8.*

"I will conquer that child, no matter what it may cost him!" boasts the misguided parent. But suppose the parent should say, "I will help that child to conquer himself, no matter what it may cost me."

—*Patterson Du Bois.*

August Eleventh

If I could mend a broken cart to-day,
  To-morrow make a kite to reach the sky,—
There is no woman in God's world could say
  She was more blissfully content than I.
But, ah! the dainty pillow next my own
  Is never rumpled by a shining head;
My singing birdling from its nest has flown:
  The little boy I used to love is dead!

—*Mary Riley Smith.*

August Twelfth

It is only necessary to watch a two-year-old closely to see what members of the family are giving him his personal "copy," to find out whether he sees his mother constantly and his father seldom; whether he plays with other children, and what their dispositions are to a degree; whether he is growing to be a person of subjection, equality or tyranny; whether he is assimilating the elements of some unorganized social content from his foreign nurse. For, in Leibnitz's phrase, the boy or girl is a social nomad, a little world, which reflects the whole system of influences coming to stir the sensibility, and just in so far as his sensibilities are stirred, he imitates and forms habits of imitating and habits,—they are character!

—*James Mark Baldwin.*

August Thirteenth

Now he laughs a little,
  And laughs,—come quick and see
My baby brother's dimples,
  As cunning as can be.

The angels love our baby,
  He is so very fair;
And so they came and kissed him
  And left the dimples there.

—*Eugene Field.*

August Fourteenth

Love is delicate; "Love is hurt with jar and fret," and you might as well expect a violin to remain in tune if roughly used, as Love to survive if chilled or driven into itself. But what a pleasure to keep it alive by:

"Little, nameless, unremembered acts
Of kindness and of love."

—*Sir John Lubbock.*

August Fifteenth

In praise of little children I will say
God first made man, then found a better way
For woman, but his third way was the best.
Of all created things the loveliest
And most divine are children. Nothing here
Can be to us more gracious or more dear.
And though when God saw all His works were good
There was no rosy flower of babyhood;
'Twas said of children in a later day
That none could enter heaven save such as they.

—*William Canton.*

August Sixteenth

Maternal love! Thou word that sums all bliss.

—*Robert Pollock.*

How *could* anything compare
With a baby fresh and fair?
How *could* God's work, pure and fine,
Ever harmonize with mine?

—*Mary Riley Smith.*

August Seventeenth

My little son, who looked from thoughtful eyes,
And moved and spoke in quiet grown-up wise,
Having my law the seventh time disobeyed,
I struck him, and dismissed
With hard words, and unkissed,—
His mother, who was patient, being dead.
Then, fearing lest his grief should hinder sleep,
I visited his bed,
But found him slumbering deep,
With darkened eyelids, and their lashes yet
From his late sobbing, wet.
And I, with moan,
Kissing away his tears, left others of my own;
For, on a table drawn beside his head,
He had put, within his reach,
A box of counters and a red-veined stone,
A piece of glass abraded by the beach,
And six or seven shells,
A bottle with bluebells
And two French copper coins, ranged there with
Careful art.
To comfort his sad heart.

—Coventry Patmore.

August Eighteenth

How silent it is,—childhood! The children,—how noisy they are! Inquisitive and garrulous, they are sometimes out of tune; laughter runs riot with them, and their sudden shrieks and prolonged crying disturb and alarm the neighbourhood. How roistering, boisterous they are,—the children! Yet how silent it is,—childhood! The very word "infant" means "speechless," and every child remains an infant, in one degree or another, long after the period of so-called infancy is past.

—*Patterson Du Bois.*

August Nineteenth

See to it that your boys and girls, when they grow up, do not remember you as an anxious, worried, irritable mother; but live such a trustful life before them that they will have always a picture of peace and trust when they think of you.

—*Hannah Whitall Smith.*

August Twentieth

Wal how could I help it, now, dearie,
If while I stood thinkin'—that day
Of the forms and the sweet baby faces
So long, oh, so long passed away.
These foolish old eyes of mine weakened,
And at last I jest dropped my head,
And givin' a sob I couldn't keep back,
"Oh, babies! *My* babies!" I said.

"Only jest for one minit to see ye
A-lyin' so merry and bright,
And waitin' for mammy to kiss ye,
My darlin's, for sweet good-night!
Only jest for one hour of havin'
Ye all to myself once more!
I'd love ye, I'd kiss ye, my babies,
As never I kissed ye afore!"

—*Mary D. Brine.*

August Twenty-first

So pure is my child, that I dare to say
His Maker would not despise
To colour the sky on some rare June day,
From the blue in his handsome eyes;
And this is the sweetest thought there can be—
This beautiful boy belongs to me.

—*Mary Riley Smith.*

August Twenty-second

God made mothers before He made ministers: the progress of Christ's kingdom depends more upon the influence of faithful, wise and pious mothers than upon any other human agency. My mother's discipline was loving but thorough; she never bribed me to good conduct with sugar plums; she praised every commendable deed heartily, for she held that an ounce of honest praise is often worth more than many pounds of punishment.

—*Theodore Cuyler.*

August Twenty-third

Monarchs whose kingdom no man bounds,
 No leagues uphold, no conquest spreads,
Whose thrones are any mossy mounds,
 Whose crowns are curls on sunny heads.

No tyrant so hard-hearted known
 Can their diplomacy resist,
They can usurp his very throne,
 He abdicates when he is kissed.

—*Helen Hunt.*

August Twenty-fourth

Thy wife shall be as a fruitful vine by the sides of thine house: thy children like olive plants round about thy table.

—*Psalm 128 : 3.*

I love these little people; and it is not a slight thing when they, who are so fresh from God, love us.

—*Charles Dickens.*

August Twenty-fifth

Come to me, O ye children!
  And whisper in my ear
What the birds and the winds are singing
  In your sunny atmosphere.

For what are all our contriving
  And the wisdom of our books,
When compared with your caresses,
  And the gladness of your looks?

Ye are better than all the ballads
  That ever were sung or said;
For ye are living poems,
  And all the rest are dead.

—*H. W. Longfellow.*

August Twenty-sixth

Hail, reverend pastors, doctors, licentiates, superintendents! Hail! most noble, most prudent, most learned lords, consuls, prætors, judges, prefects, chancellors, secretaries, magistrates, professors, etc. I am not jesting: my speech is serious: for I look on these little boys, not as they are now, but a view to the purpose of the Divine mind, on account of which they are delivered to us for instruction.

—*Philip Melanchthon.*

August Twenty-seventh

No mother has an easy time, and most mothers have very hard times, and yet what true mother would barter her experience of joy and sorrow in exchange for a life of cold selfishness, which insists upon perpetual amusement and the avoidance of care and which often finds its fit dwelling-place in some flat designed to furnish with the least possible expenditure of effort the maximum of comfort and of luxury, but in which there is literally no place for children?

—*Theodore Roosevelt.*

August Twenty-eighth

Observe how soon, and to what a degree, this influence begins to operate! Her first ministration for her infant is to enter, as it were, the valley of the shadow of death, and win its life at the peril of her own! How different must an affection thus founded be from all others!

—*Lydia H. Sigourney.*

There is perhaps no such moment of exquisite joy, of deep unutterable thanksgiving taking the place of pain and sorrow as when a woman knows herself to be the living mother of a living child.

—*Andrew Murray.*

August Twenty-ninth

Pure hearted little innocents! Compared with older people, whom we endure, how great thy faith and how few thy faults!

John Habberton.

The sweet safe corner of the household fire
Behind the heads of children.

—*Anon.*

August Thirtieth

I have watched this matter carefully in the lives of several children I have known, and I have continually found that their worst naughtinesses are plainly induced and developed, either directly or indirectly, by the grown-up people who have the care of them. Their antagonism is roused by harshness, or injustice, or want of consideration, or ridicule, and then they are punished for the naughtiness we ourselves have actually created.

—Hannah Whitall Smith.

August Thirty-first

Softly—sadly—slowly—the toys crept round the floor.
"It's been a week since we've seen our king," said a drum, "yes, even more."
"I wonder what has become of him," said a rolling rubber ball.
"I haven't seen him since the day he, trembling, let me fall."
"Sad," said a sword, and "Sad," said a flag, and "Sad," said a gun of wood.
"Sad," spoke a rocking hobby-horse as sad as hobby could.

And all of the nursery toys crept up to the nursery
window-sill;
And there they whispered in soft, low tones, for the
room was very still.

But they waited and waited, and then a cloud stole
stealthily over the sky
As a nurse stepped in with a picture-book, and laid
it down with a sigh.
And when she'd gone, the toys all crowded up to
the book and said:—
"Where's our king? does he not like us as well as
his Christmas sled?"
But the picture-book turned sadly round and spoke
to the nursery land:—
"'Tis I that's been with the king for days; I was
held in his little hand;—
And then the nurse came quietly and carried me
slowly away,
And a mother knelt by a trundle-bed,—and that is
all that I can say."

And oh, 'twas still in that nursery room; very, very
still.
Still for another long, long day,—and a day and a
night,—until
There floated up through the winding hall, a singing soft and low;
Music the toys had never heard, solemn and sad
and slow.

And they tiptoed up to the window-pane of that little nursery-room;
And watched the snowflakes falling, and peered through the snowy gloom;
And they didn't know why the children stood in the yard and street near by,
And they didn't know why they all looked sad and many were seen to cry.

But now a nursery is filled with toys that wait for a little king,
And they've scarcely stirred since the day they heard the people sing,
But they lie there still on the nursery floor, and softly whisper then:—
"Where's our king? has he gone away from his little, soldier men?"
Yet no one answers their grievous cries; and no one hears their say,—
For the little king rules on a golden throne, miles and miles away.

—*Allen Ayrault Green.*

The Month of September

September First

One of the greatest differences between the fairies and us is that they never do anything useful. When the first baby laughed for the first time, his laugh broke into a million pieces, and they all went skipping about. That was the beginning of fairies.

—*J. M. Barrie.*

(From "The Little White Bird," by courtesy of Charles Scribner's Sons, Publishers.)

September Second

Look at him; pick him up in his long, white gown; he may have an excess of colour,—but such a pretty colour! He is a little pouty about the mouth, —but such a mouth! His hair is a little scant, and he is rather wandering in the eye; but, Good Heavens, what an eye!

—*Donald G. Mitchell.*

We should treat children as God does us, who makes us happiest when He leaves us under the influence of innocent delusions.

—*Goethe.*

September Third

They tell me the world is a dreary place,
  And heavily sown with tears;
But when I look in my child's dear face,
  My heart is too glad for fears;
Glad, as the good Lord meant me to be,
When He gave this beautiful boy to me.

—*Mary Riley Smith.*

September Fourth

Oh, when a mother meets on high,
The babe she lost in infancy,
Hath she not then for pains and fears,
  The day of woe, the watchful night,
For all her sorrow, all her tears,
  An over-payment of delight?

—*Robert Southey.*

September Fifth

The mother can clothe him in Jaeger wool from head to foot, or keep him in low neck, short sleeves and low stockings, because she thinks it pretty; she can feed him exclusively on raw beef, or on vegetables, or on cereals; she can give him milk to drink, or let him sip his father's beer and wine; put him to bed at sundown, or keep him up till midnight; teach him the catechism and the thirty-nine articles, or tell him there is no God; she can cram him with facts before he has any appetite or power of assimilation, or she can make a fool of him. She can dose him with old-school remedies, or she can let him die without remedies because she doesn't believe in the reality of disease. She is quite willing to legislate for his stomach, his mind, his soul, his teachableness, it goes without saying, being generally in inverse proportion to her knowledge, for the arrogance of science is humility compared with the pride of ignorance.

—*Kate Douglas Wiggin.*

September Sixth

I believe more and more, as I grow older, that a large part of our contests with children are wasted, and that patience and tact would commonly accomplish the same end, without the crossing of bayonets. The wisest and most successful parents seem to me those who take this into account, who reduce direct contests to a minimum, bend the twig instead of breaking it, divert the course of the torrent instead of trying to dam it up.

—*Hannah Whitall Smith.*

September Seventh

What do they say in Baby-land?
Why, the oddest things;
Might as well
Try to tell
What the birdie sings.

Who is the Queen of Baby-land?
Mother, kind and sweet;
And her love
Born above,
Guides the little feet.

—*Eugene Field.*

September Eighth

In praising or loving a child, we love and praise not that which is, but that which we hope for.

—*Goethe.*

Aye, these young things lie safe in our hearts just so
long
As their wings are in growing; and when these are
strong
They break it, and farewell! the bird flies.

—*Owen Meredith.*

September Ninth.

I almost think the angels
Who tread life's garden fair,
Drop down the sweet wild blossoms
That bloom around us there.

It seems a breath from heaven
Round many a cradle lies,
And every little baby
Is a message from the skies.

—*Anon.*

September Tenth

Last night a babe awakened,
  And, babe, how strange and new
Must seem the home and people
  The stork has brought you to;
And yet, methinks you like them,—
  You neither stare nor weep,
But closer to my dear one
  You cuddle, and you sleep.

Last night my heart grew fonder—
  O happy heart of mine,
Sing of the inspirations
  That round my pathway shine!
And sing your sweetest love-song
  To this dear nestling wee
The Stork from 'Way-Out-Yonder
  Hath brought to mine and me!

—*Eugene Field.*

(From "Love Songs of Childhood," by courtesy of the publishers, Charles Scribner's Sons.)

September Eleventh

As children harrowed by fantastic dreams
  Cry sharply in the night for some dear hand
  To hold their own,—for some brave form to stand
Beside their couch and crowd away what seems
So real and so terrific a shape,—
  And through the dark there comes with eager speed
  The unerring touch that answers to their need,
The voice that charges terror make escape;
So we are wont to piteously call,
When awful blackness closes us about,
  With every room inhabited by fear,
And He who marks a single sparrow's fall,
Regarding more His children, reaches out,
  And bids each cruel phantom disappear.

—Elizabeth Gallup Perkins.

September Twelfth

Jesus saith to Simon Peter, Lovest thou Me more than these? He saith unto Him, Yea, Lord, Thou knowest that I love Thee. He saith unto him, Feed My lambs.

—John 21 : 15.

A mother's love, the best love; God's love, the highest love.

—German.

September Thirteenth

The twig is so easily bended,
 I have banished the rule and the rod,
I have taught them the goodness of knowledge,
 They have taught me the goodness of God.
My heart is a dungeon of darkness,
 Where I shut them from breaking a rule;
My frown is sufficient correction;
 My love is the law of the school.

—*Charles M. Dickenson.*

September Fourteenth

Who may not see that a child lies under so many restrictions, on account of its natural weakness, as to acknowledge it barbarous to add to this restraint that of our caprices? . . . How subject are those who judge precipitately of children to be egregiously deceived! They often betray, in this, less judgment than the children of whom they judge.

—*Jean J. Rousseau.*

September Fifteenth

I know that the coffin was narrow and small,
One yard would have served for an ample pall;
And one man in his arms could have borne away
The rosewood and its freight of clay;
But I know that darling hopes were hid
Beneath that little coffin-lid.

I know that some things were hid away,
The crimson frock and wrapping gay;
The little sock and the half-worn shoe,
The cap with its plumes and tassels blue;
And an empty crib, with its covers spread,
As white as the face of the sinless dead.

—*Anon.*

September Sixteenth

God could not be everywhere, and so He made mothers.

—*Anon.*

Love is a bird that sings in the heart of a woman.

—*Alphonse Karr.*

But the love of children is like some rare heavenly air
That makes long Indian summers there.

—*J. T. Trowbridge.*

September Seventeenth

Who owns the child? If the parent owns him, mind, body and soul, we must adopt one line of argument; if, as a human being, he owns himself, we must adopt another. In my thought the parent is simply a divinely appointed guardian, who acts for his child until he attains what we call the age of discretion,—that highly uncertain period which arrives very late in life with some persons, and not at all with others.

—*Kate Douglas Wiggin.*

September Eighteenth

The instruction received at the mother's knee and the paternal lessons, together with the pious and sweet souvenirs of the fireside, are never effaced entirely from the soul.

—*Robert de Lamennais.*

Sweet is the smile of home,—the mutual look,
  When hearts are of each other sure;
Sweet all the joys that crowd the household nook,
  The haunt of all affections pure.

—*John Keble.*

September Nineteenth

Sleep, little baby of mine,
 Night and the darkness are near;
Jesus looks down through the shadows that frown,
 And baby has nothing to fear;
Shut little sleepy blue eyes,
 Dear little head, be at rest;
Jesus, like you, was a baby once too,
 And slept on His own mother's breast.
  Lullaby, Lullaby,
  Sleep, my baby, sleep.

Sleep, little baby of mine,
 Soft on your pillow of white;
Jesus is here to watch over you, dear,
 And nothing can harm you to-night;
Oh, little darling of mine,
 What can you know of the bliss,
The comfort I keep, awake and asleep,
 Because I am certain of this.
  Lullaby, Lullaby,
  Sleep, my baby, sleep.

—*Anon.*

September Twentieth

But what mother's sufferings were ever equal to Mary's? Jesus was only thirty-three, her first-born, the son of her strength. There He hung before her eyes, but she was helpless. His wounds bled, but she dared not staunch them; His mouth was parched, but she could not moisten it. These outstretched arms used to clasp her neck; she used to fondle these pierced hands and feet. Ah! the nails pierced her as well as Him; the thorns round His brow were a circle of flame about her heart; the taunts flung at Him wounded her likewise.

—*James Stalker.*

September Twenty-first

A babe in a house is a well-spring of pleasure,
A messenger of peace and love;
A resting-place for innocence on earth,
A link between angels and men.

—*Martin Farquhar Tupper.*

A sweet, new blossom of Humanity,
Fresh fallen from God's own home to flower on earth.

—*Geraid Massey.*

September Twenty-second

It is said there are three types of women. The most numerous are the natural mothers, whose instincts are overwhelmingly maternal; the next are the women who are better wives than mothers, and the last are the rare women equally fit in either capacity.

—*Ellis Meredith.*

September Twenty-third

We are all here,
Father, mother,
Sister, brother.

You that I love with love so dear,
This may not long of us be said;
Soon must we join the gathered dead,
And by the hearth we now sit round,
Some other circle will be found.

Oh, then, that wisdom may we know,
Which yields a life of peace below!
So in the world which follows this,
May each repeat in words of bliss,
"We're all—all here!"

—*Charles Sprague.*

September Twenty-fourth

" Glad I am home ! " It is the cry
 That many a weary wanderer gives,
 When tired of the life he lives
He turns him to the wall to die.
And as I to my joyous breast
 Took back my truant child that day,
 So will the arms that live for aye
Receive each truant soul to rest.

—*Eugene Field.*

September Twenty-fifth

" I believe if my papa and mama had stayed away any longer, I believe I would die. I've been so lonesome for 'em that I haven't known what to do ;—I've cried whole pillowfuls about it, right here in the dark." " When I gets lonesome," said Budge, " it feels as if my mouth was all tied up, an' a great big stone was right in here." And Budge put his hand on his chest.

—*John Habberton.*

September Twenty-sixth

Mothers are the oniy goddesses in whom the whole world believes.

—*Anon.*

At first babies feed on the mother's bosom, but always on her heart.

—*Henry Ward Beecher.*

September Twenty-seventh

Here's the little coat, but oh!
Where is he, we've censured so!
Don't you hear us calling, dear?
Back! Come back, and never fear.
You may wander where you will,
Over orchard, field and hill;
You may kill the birds, or do
Anything that pleases you!
Ah, this empty coat of his!
Every tatter worth a kiss;
Every stain as pure instead
As the white stars overhead;
And the pocket-homes were they
Of the little hands that play
Now no more,—but absent, thus
Beckon us.

—*James Whitcomb Riley.*

(Used by special permission of the publishers, The Bobbs-Merrill Company, from "Rhymes of Childhood," copyrighted, 1900.)

September Twenty-eighth

He was logical, I was illogical; he was true, I was false; he was doing his best, I was doing my worst. I had imposed conditions which could not be complied with; I had exacted a promise which he was too innocent, too inexperienced to know that he could not keep. I reflected upon him as morally disobedient, when he was only physically fallible; as obstinate, when he was only confused and embarrassed; careless, when he was only bewildered; heedless, when he was only hurried; false, when he was truest to himself and to me; wrong, when his best wish and motive was to be right.

—Patterson Du Bois.

September Twenty-ninth

The grandmother lifted her darling,
  And patted his head on her breast,
And sang in a tremulous treble,
  Till all Bobby's woes were at rest.
And so the wee whip, bright and yellow,
  Was laid on the mantel again,—
And that is the way that the grandmas
  Spoil nine little boys out of ten.

—Mary Riley Smith.

September Thirtieth

The destiny of the nation lies far more in the hands of women,—the mothers—than in the hands of those who possess power or those who are innovators, who seldom understand themselves. *We must cultivate women,* who are educators of the human race, else a new generation cannot accomplish its task.

—*Froebel.*

The Month of

October First

Beautiful child, may'st thou soar above,
A warbling cherub of joy and love;
A drop on eternity's mighty sea,
A blossom of life's immortal tree;
Floating, flowering forevermore,
In the blessed light of the golden shore.
And as I gaze on thy sinless bloom
And thy radiant face, they dispel my gloom;
I feel He will keep thee undefiled,
And His love protect my beautiful child.

—*W. A. H. Sigourney.*

October Second

The eldest of the three was a woman in that season of life when the early autumn gives to the summer leaves a warmer glow, yet fades them not. Though the mother of many children, she was still beautiful,—resembling those trees which blossom in October, when the leaves are changing, and whose fruit and blossom are on the branch at once.

—*H. W. Longfellow.*

October Third

All Gracious, grant to those who bear
A mother's charge, the strength and light,
To lead the steps that own their care
In ways of Love and Truth and Right.

—*Bryant.*

Alone
She moves, the queen of her own quiet home.

—*Mark Trafton.*

October Fourth

I know that some good nurses point with triumph to infants "who give no trouble," who will allow themselves to be laid in the cradles and fall asleep, who are "spoiled" by no rocking or over much dandling. But I maintain that the traditional lullaby is the natural satisfaction of a natural craving, and cannot be abandoned without proportionate harm. "Love is essential to an infant's well-being, a babe is fed with milk and praise," tender Charles Lamb reminds us,—and the mother naturally manifests hers in brooding over it, in giving up time to it in rocking and moving, and soothing her child in manifold ways; and if "beauty born of murmuring sound shall pass into 'its' face," how much more subtly shall love pass into the spiritual seedling and nurture it into ampler life?

—*Mrs. Frank Malleson.*

October Fifth

Beautiful child, to thy look is given
A gleam serene,—not of earth, but of heaven;
With thy tell-tale eyes and prattling tongue,
Would thou could'st ever thus be young.
Like the liquid strain of the mockingbird,
From stair to hall thy voice is heard;
How oft in the garden nooks thou'rt found,
With flowers thy curly head around!
And kneeling beside me with figure quaint,
Oh, who would not dote on my infant saint?

—*W. A. H. Sigourney.*

October Sixth

To bring a helpless babe to light,
  Then, while it lies forlorn,
To gaze upon that dearest sight,
  And feel herself new-born,
In its existence lose her own,
And live and breathe in it alone,
  This is a Mother's Love.

—*James Montgomery.*

The mother's love—there's none so pure,
  So constant and so kind;
No human passion doth endure
  Like this within the mind.

—*Anon.*

October Seventh

A child does not carve epitaphs nor build monuments, nor pen memorials; he seeks not relief through conscious expression or deliberate display of grief. He pleads not for sympathy through conventionalities,—the dress of mourning, the isolation from society, the darkened house, the silenced musical instrument. He is innocent of the adult's tormenting affliction of showing by prescribed rules that he is afflicted. The child carries his hurt out into the sunshine, that it may get some life out of the light.

—*Patterson Du Bois.*

October Eighth

How sensitive are grown-up people to ridicule! How it mortifies and rankles and embitters! They would sooner take any affront than to be laughed at. Yet with what frequency are children made the subject of ridicule. Perhaps in company or at table, a child makes a remark, or uses a phrase which to the grown-up people, with their superior knowledge, contains an element of absurdity. Instantly there is a burst of laughter, and the poor child is filled with mortification and distress, and then, probably, is scolded for being sulky.

—*Hannah Whitall Smith.*

October Ninth

'Twas the dear little girl that I scolded—
  "For was it a moment like this,"
I said, "when she knew I was busy
  To come romping in for a kiss?—
Come rowdying up from her mother,
  And clamouring there at my knee,
For 'one 'ittle kiss for my dolly,
  And one 'ittle uzzer for me!'"

God pity the heart that repelled her,
  And the cold hand that turned her away!
And take, from the lips that denied her,
  This answerless prayer of to-day!
Take, Lord, from my mem'ry forever,
  That pitiful sob of despair,
And the patter and trip of the little bare feet
  And the one piercing cry of despair!

—*James Whitcomb Riley.*

October Tenth

I know of no worse sin than bringing an unwelcome child into the world, save the birth of one stamped with hereditary disease.

—Ellis Meredith.

My laddie, oh, my laddie, I am wistful as I clasp
Your dimpled hand within my own and think how many men
Gone far from earth and memory, beyond our mortal grasp,
Are living and are breathing, dear child, in you again.

—Quoted by Margaret Sangster.

October Eleventh

Theirs is the language of the heavens, the power,
The thought, the image, the silent joy;
Words are but undergarments in their souls;
When they are grasping with their greatest strength
They do not breathe among them.

—William Wordsworth.

The lesson for parents is so difficult, being continually giving, without always finding the return.

—Princess Alice of Hesse.

October Twelfth

Her child must go out into the world and fight his battles alone; but she can arm him with the armour of good habits, place upon his head the helmet of rational self-determination, put into his hand the sword of inspiration, and above all, give to him the shield of faith and reverence, so that he goes forth ready to defy the demon's appetite within and the devils of temptation without. She need not fear to send her son forth, or tremble for her daughter's happiness;—they have begun aright and the law of continuity will keep them aright, unless some mighty force hurl them for a moment from the path of rectitude, and even then the reaction will swing them back into the accustomed path.

—*Elizabeth Harrison.*

October Thirteenth

Beginning with obedience, the parent has to lead the child on to liberty; the apparent opposites have to be reconciled in practice; really to choose and will for himself what his parent wills, to find his happiness not only in the obedience to the parents' commands, but in the approval of the thing commanded,—this is what the child must be forced to. And here is indeed the highest art, the real difficulty of training a child in the way he should go.

—*Andrew Murray.*

October Fourteenth

" How many are you, then," said I,
  " If they two are in heaven ? "
The little maiden did reply,
  " Oh, Master, we are seven !

" But they are dead,—those two are dead,
  Their spirits are in heaven."

'Twas throwing words away, for still
The little maid would have her will,
  And said, " Nay, we are seven."

—*William Wordsworth.*

October Fifteenth

A mother is a mother still,
  The holiest thing alive.

—*Samuel Taylor Coleridge.*

If the whole world were put into one scale and my mother in the other, the world would kick the beam.

—*Lord Landdomes.*

If there be aught surpassing human deed or word or thought, it is a mother's love.

—*Marchioness de Spadora.*

October Sixteenth

The woman who takes into her heart her own children may be a very ordinary woman, but the woman who takes into her heart the children of others,—she is one of God's mothers.

—*Anon.*

Of such the kingdom!—Teach Thou us,
  O Master most Divine,
To feel the deep significance
  Of these wise words of Thine!

—*J. G. Whittier.*

October Seventeenth

Oh, do not read to me of the campaigns of Cæsar; tell me nothing about Napoleon's wonderful exploits. I tell you that as God and angels look down upon the silent history of that woman's administration, and upon those men-building processes which went on in her heart and mind through a score of years, nothing external, no outward development of kingdoms, no empire building can compare with what she has done.

—*H. W. Beecher.*

October Eighteenth

O baby, with your marvellous eyes,
  Clear as the yet unfallen dew,
Methinks you are the only wise,
No change can touch you with surprise,—
  Nothing is strange or new to you.

O shield me with your light caress,
  Dear heart, so stainless and so new!
Unconscious of your loveliness,
Your beauty, fresh and shadowless,
  As is a violet of its blue.

—*Elizabeth Akers Allen.*

October Nineteenth

We must therefore cultivate mothers.

—*Froebel.*

That our sons may be as plants grown up in their
  youth,
That our daughters may be as corner-stones,
Polished after the similitude of a palace;
Happy is that people that is in such a case;
Yea, happy is that people whose God is the Lord.

—*Psalm 144: 12, 15.*

October Twentieth

In dealing with children we must always remember that they can never be judged by a jury of their peers. Their standpoint is not that of grown-up people, and one cannot wonder that their standards are different. Often they do not in the least comprehend what the grown-up standards are. Even the words used by their caretakers are utterly misunderstood by them.

A little girl suffered untold distress from the reproofs of her conscience at being obliged to sing the hymn, "Nearer, my God, to Thee," because she thought it was, "Nero, my God, to Thee," and it seemed to her so dreadful to sing a hymn to such a wicked man as Nero, and to call him God!

—Hannah Whitall Smith.

October Twenty-first

"For my child's sake," is the only parental motto that will bring the child to adopt "For my parents' sake" as his motto. The only principle that works under all conditions is,—not the principle of arbitrary parental mastery, but of parental aid and service.

—Patterson Du Bois.

October Twenty-second

Tenderly enough
Has God's sweet mercy through His smiting shone,
Young feet are tender, and the way is rough;
Be glad that you can tread the thorns alone.

It is not long. The way is short between,
And we are near the gates of pearl and gold,
And yonder rise the hills of living green,
Where children never die, nor yet grow old!

And when the storms shall beat and rains shall fall,
And when you faint beneath the sun's fierce ray,
O friend, be glad! and sing above it all,
"My child is safe from all these ills to-day!"

—*Mary Riley Smith.*

October Twenty-third

Love suffereth long and is kind; seeketh not her own, is not easily provoked.

—*1 Corinthians 13 : 4, 5.*

After all, love is the most indispensable element in the relation between parent and child. It is lucky it is so common, for raising the families without it is hard work and ill done. The great detail in which parents most excel institutions in bringing up children is that they love them more.

—*E. S. Martin.*

October Twenty-fourth

Be cautious, be careful and thoughtful at this point, O parents! You can here at one blow destroy, at least for a long time, the instincts of formative activity in your children, if you repel their help as childish, useless, of little avail, or even as a hindrance.

—*Froebel.*

October Twenty-fifth

At God's right hand sits one *who was a child,*
Born as the humblest, and who here abode
Till our sorrow He had suffered all.
They now who weep, remember that He wept.
The tempted, the despised, the sorrowing, feel
That Jesus, too, drank of these cups of woe.
And oh, if our joys be tasted less,—
If all but one passed from His lips away,—
That one,—a mother's love—by His partaking,
Is like a thread of heaven spun through our life,
And we in the untiring watch, the tears,
The tenderness and the fond trust of a mother,
May feel a heavenly closeness unto God,—
For such, all human in its best excess,
Was Mary's love for Jesus.

—*N. P. Willis.*

October Twenty-sixth

I cannot now name any time, day or place when I was converted. It was my faithful mother's steady and constant influence that led me gradually along, and I grew into a religious life under her potent training, and by the power of the Holy Spirit working through her agency. I feel now that the happy fifty-six years that I have spent in the glorious ministry of the Gospel of redemption is the direct outcome of that beloved mother's prayers, teaching, example, and holy influence.

—*Theodore Cuyler.*

October Twenty-seventh

Motherhood is priced
Of God, at price no man may dare
To lessen or misunderstand.
The motherhood which came
To virgin sets in vestal flame,
Fed by each new-born infant's hand,
With heaven's air,
With heaven's food,
The crown of purest purity revealed,
Virginity eternal signed and sealed
Upon all motherhood!

—*Helen Hunt Jackson.*

October Twenty-eighth

Truly there is nothing in the world so blessed or so sweet as the heritage of children.

—Mrs. Oliphant.

Whenever we step out of domestic life in search of felicity, we come back again, disappointed, tired, and chagrined. One day passed under our own roof, with our family, is worth a thousand in another place.

—Earl of Orrery.

October Twenty-ninth

Children have more need of models than of critics.

—Joseph Joubert.

Every home with its parents and children presents a problem of love which only the spirit of quietness can solve.

—J. R. Miller.

Believe me, sir, it is better to mourn ten children dead than one living, and I have buried many.

—Susanna Wesley (Letter to her brother).

October Thirtieth

I never dreamed that God could need
  A child so small as this;
I quite forgot, until God spoke,
  That this, my child, was His.
I said, "My child shall dwell with me
  From life's dawn till life's even,"
But God replied, "The child is Mine,
  And he shall dwell in heaven."

Here is the cradle where he lay
  White as his innocence;
No hand hath touched it since the day
  God stopped and took him thence.
Father of the Beloved Son
  To earthly exile given,
Thou knowest—may Thy will be done—
  I have a child in heaven.

—*W. J. Dawson.*

October Thirty-first

In Sparta, when a boy committed a crime, his father was punished. And to-day, if strict justice were done, there would be thousands of parents exchanging places with their children in reformatories or jails; or, to come closer home, it is probably the mother or the nurse who many a time ought to be standing in the corner instead of the child.

—*Hannah Whitall Smith.*

The Month of

November First

Two small brown hands, unsoiled by sin,
  Are folded softly on my knee,
And over them my child's dear head
  Is bowed in sweet humility.

Hark to the little honest prayer!
  " Dear God, I am too tired to pray,
And 'tain't as if you didn't know
  Just all I've said and done to-day.

" I know it takes a sight of love
  To make a boy's sins white, but then
You don't go back on what you say,
  And I am not afraid. Amen."

—*Mary Riley Smith.*

November Second

The world does once in a while recognize the hero in a child who rescues a comrade from some bodily peril. But of the struggles within, the fierce spiritual combats for the mastery of right over wrong, for the overcoming of difficulties of temperament, difficulties in the constitution of mind and body, difficulties of environment,—of these the world keeps itself ignorant, and the child knows it and feels it. Yet all the nobler is its heroism for this isolation, this painful loneliness, this cruel exile of the soul.

—*Patterson Du Bois.*

November Third

Take heed that ye despise not one of these little ones, for I say unto you, that in heaven their angels do always behold the face of My Father which is in heaven.

How think ye? If a man have an hundred sheep and one of them be gone astray, doth he not leave the ninety and nine and goeth into the mountains and seeketh that which is gone astray? And if so be that he find it, verily I say unto you, he rejoiceth more of that sheep than of the ninety and nine which went not astray.

Even so it is not the will of your Father which is in heaven that one of these little ones should perish.

—*Matthew 18: 10–14.*

November Fourth

Planning for the little people,
  That they may grow brave and true;
Active brain and busy fingers,
While the precious seedtime lingers,
Guiding, guarding, hoping, fearing,
Waiting for the harvest nearing,—
    This is what the mothers do.

Playing with the little people
  Sweet old games forever new,
Coaxing, cuddling, cooing, kissing,
Baby's every grief dismissing,
Laughing, sighing, soothing, singing,
While the happy days are winging,—
    This is what the mothers do.

—Mary L. C. Robinson.

November Fifth

We think even a poor mother strangely careless if she does not provide shelter and clothes. But how more than equally necessary it is that she should, in addition to material comforts, prepare herself to receive the coming gift! If the loveliness and holiness of such gifts were not obscured to ordinary vision by their commonness, could parents ever receive them without befitting humility and reverence?

—Mrs. Frank Malleson

November Sixth

Children don't need to be made happy; a healthy child is, of itself, a happy being; its joy in existence is the prerogative of its youth.

—*Ennes Richmond.*

Sleep, baby, sleep,
Thy Saviour loves His sheep;
He is the Lamb of God on high
Who for our sakes came down to die,
Sleep, baby, sleep.

—*Elizabeth Prentiss.*

November Seventh

A child's soul is more tender and vulnerable than the finest or tenderest plant, and a cross look or a rough touch or an unkind tone is often sufficient to inflict a savage blow. God grant that every mother may recognize in time the sacredness and tenderness of the soul of her child!

—*Hannah Whitall Smith.*

November Eighth

Mother, O mother! forever I cry for you,
  Sing the old song I may never forget;
Even in slumber I murmur and sigh for you,—
    Mother, O mother,
  Sing low, "Little brother,
  Sleep, for thy mother bends over thee yet!"

Mother, O mother! the years are so lonely,
  Filled but with weariness, doubt and regret!
Can't you come back to me, for to-night only,
    Mother, my mother,
  And sing, "Little brother,
  Sleep, for thy mother bends over thee yet!"

Mother, O mother! must longing and sorrow
  Leave me in darkness, with eyes ever wet
And never the hope of a meeting to-morrow?
    Answer me, mother,
  And sing, "Little brother,
  Sleep, for thy mother bends over thee yet!"

—*James Whitcomb Riley.*

November Ninth

All your dimpled palms have brought her
From God's world of far away;
All your baby-lisp has taught her,
Mother scarcely dares to say,
Knowing how the great God blessed her
When He sent you here to stay.

For His sunshine and your kisses
Seem to melt and mix and grow
Perfected. Mere summer misses
Something of your mouth's ripe glow,
Scarlet duller far than this is
Do the poppied corn-fields show.

All the rapture, all the pleasure,
Lovers chaunt and poets sing
Are outweighed by the full measure
Of this far more perfect thing.
For a child's prayer angels treasure
As they soar on radiant wing.

Dear, the wealth of all the roses
Cannot match the sweets untold
Of your fair thoughts, fairer posies,
Mine to gather, tend and hold,
Praising God night, noon and morning,
For my baby's heart of gold.

—*May Bateman.*

November Tenth

Books cannot teach what toys inculcate. Choose his toys wisely and then leave him alone with them. The toy at this period is surrounded with a halo of poetry and mystery, and lays hold of the imagination and the heart without awakening vulgar curiosity. Thrice happy age when one can hug one's white woolly lamb to one's bibbed breast, kiss its pink bead eyes in irrational ecstasy and manipulate the squeak in its foreground without desire to explore the cause thereof!

—*Kate Douglas Wiggin.*

November Eleventh

In that holy time of mystery, when mother and child are still one, and influences from a mother's spirit pass into the child, God says, "Of all that I said unto the woman, let her beware; all that I commanded her, let her observe."

—*Andrew Murray.*

November Twelfth

Lingering still in the twilight gray,
After the radiance fades away,
I watch my darling, so still, so fair,
With thankful heart that to my care,
  For happiness
  No words express
Awhile God trusts a gift so dear.

As in his little bed I place
My babe, in all his slumbering grace,
Heaven's starry lamps are lit on high,
One, angel borne, now flashes by,
  And by their light
  Through all the night,
Celestial watchers will be nigh.

—*Eugene Field.*

November Thirteenth

Sometimes in the dusk of evening
  I only shut my eyes,
And the children are all about me,
  A vision from the skies;
The babes whose dimpled fingers
  Lost the way to my breast,
And the beautiful ones, the angels,
  Passed to the world of the blest.

—*Margaret Sangster.*

November Fourteenth

When the morning, half in shadow,
Ran along the hill and meadow,
And with milk-white fingers parted
Christmas roses, golden-hearted,
Opening over ruins hoary,
Every purple morning-glory;
And, outshaking from the bushes,
Singing larks and pleasant thrushes,
That's the time our little baby
Strayed from Paradise, it may be;
Came with eyes like heaven above her;
O we could not choose but love her!

—*Phœbe Cary.*

November Fifteenth

But the angel said unto him, Fear not, Zacharias, for thy prayer is heard; and thy wife Elizabeth shall bear thee a son, and thou shalt call his name John. And thou shalt have joy and gladness; and many shall rejoice at his birth. For he shall be great in the sight of the Lord and shall drink neither wine nor strong drink; and he shall be filled with the Holy Ghost, even from his mother's womb.

—*Luke 1: 13–15.*

November Sixteenth

Many children grow up like plants under bell-glasses. They are surrounded only by artificial and prepared influences. They are house-bred, room-bred, nurse-bred, mother-bred,—everything but self-bred. The object of training is to help the child to take care of himself; but many parents use their children only as a kind of spool on which to reel off their own experience, and they are bound and corded until they perish by inanity, or break all bonds and cords and rush to ruin by reaction.

—*H. W. Beecher.*

November Seventeenth

Do you think, O blue-eyed banditti,
Because you have scaled the wall,
Such an old mustache as I am
Is not a match for you all?

I have you fast in my fortress,
And will not let you depart,
But put you down into the dungeon,
In the round tower of my heart.

And there will I keep you forever,
Yes, forever and a day,
Till the walls shall crumble to ruin
And moulder in dust away.

—*H. W. Longfellow.*

November Eighteenth

What a joy to be a father! What new emotions crowd the eye with tears, and make the hand tremble! What a benevolence radiates from you towards the nurse,—towards the physician, towards everybody! What a holiness and sanctity of love grows upon your old devotion to that wife of your bosom,—the mother of your child!

—*Donald G. Mitchell.*

November Nineteenth

I think when I read that sweet story of old,
  When Jesus was here among men,
How He called little children as lambs to His fold,
  I should like to have been with them then.

I wish that His hands had been placed on my head,
  That His arm had been thrown around me,
And that I might have seen His kind look when He said,
  "Let the little ones come unto Me."

—*Jemima Luke.*

November Twentieth

O'er wayward childhood would'st thou hold firm rule,
And sun thee in the light of happy faces?
Love, Hope and Patience,—these must be thy graces,
And in thine own heart let them first keep school.

—*Samuel Taylor Coleridge.*

And whoso shall receive one such little child in My name, receiveth Me.

—*Matthew 18 : 5.*

November Twenty-first

A truthful page is childhood's lovely face,
Whereon sweet Innocence has record made,—
And outward semblance of the young heart's grace,
Where truth, and love and trust are all portrayed.

—*Benjamin Penhallow Shillaber.*

For Jesus I trained a sweet child,
She was fair as the roses half blown;
He came to my garden and smiled,
And tenderly took back His own.

Mrs. M. A. Bigelow

November Twenty-second

Compulsion is the attempt to get a deed done where the conviction that it is right is absent.

Voluntary obedience is a deed performed after the right state of feeling towards the thing has been induced.

Compulsion is an attempt to manufacture the fruit without planting the seed.

Voluntary obedience is the fruit that is brought forth by the living plant.

A forced obedience may sometimes be necessary in an emergency, but it ought to be the exception and not the rule.

—*Hannah Whitall Smith.*

November Twenty-third

My little nephew was prowling about my sitting-room during the absence of his nurse. I was busy writing, and when he took up a delicate pearl opera-glass, I stopped his investigations with the time honoured, " No, no, dear, that's for grown-up people."

" Hasn't it got any little-boy end ? " was asked wistfully. That " little-boy " end is sometimes just what we fail to give, even when we think we are straining every nerve to surround the child with pleasures.

—*Kate Douglas Wiggin.*

November Twenty-fourth

I always think that in the end children educate the parents.

—*Princess Alice.*

A well-regulated home is a millennium on a small scale.

—*T. DeWitt Talmage.*

" God thought to give the sweetest thing
In His Almighty power
To Earth ; and deeply pondering
What it should be,—one hour
In fondest joy and love of heart
Outweighing every other,
He moved the gates of Heaven apart
And gave to Earth a mother."

November Twenty-fifth

It is impossible to estimate too highly the value and the helpfulness of a true home of love. Home is a shelter. Young lives nest there and find warmth and protection.

—*J. R. Miller.*

Above all remember that it is the love of God that is the secret of a loving home on earth.

—*Andrew Murray.*

November Twenty-sixth

If we knew the baby's fingers
  Pressed against the window-pane,
Would be cold and stiff to-morrow,—
  Never trouble us again:
Would the bright eyes of our darling
  Catch the frown upon our brow?
Would the prints of rosy fingers
  Vex us then as they do now?

Ah, these little ice-cold fingers,
  How they point our memories back
To the hasty words and actions
  Strewn along our backward track!
How those little hands remind us,
  As in snowy grace they lie,
Not to scatter thorns, but roses,
  For our reaping by and by!

—*Mary Riley Smith.*

November Twenty-seventh

And say to mothers what a holy charge
Is theirs; with what a kingly power their love
Might rule the fountains of the new-born mind.
Warn them to wake at early morn and sow
Good seed, before the world has sown its tares.

—*Mrs. L. H. Sigourney.*

November Twenty-eighth

Across the sea,
Across the sea,
Some angel's wing shall waft to me
My child, whose little hands unfold
E'en now my heart-strings in their hold;
O hour divine, when with my eyes,
I clasp my gift from Paradise!

—*Lila Munro Taintor.*

November Twenty-ninth

Let us strive to follow the ideal which our Lord Himself has given to us, in all its fullness, in all its grand proportions. Let us aim at nothing short of a life which will embrace in it all the glory of the heavens, as well as the gladness of the earth, which will put "Thou," "Thine," "Thee," in the first place, "We," "Ours," "Us," in the second.

—*Quoted by Miss Harrison.*

November Thirtieth

A baby has a right, too frequently denied it, to be let alone. It ought to be a rule in the nursery never to disturb the infant when it is happy and quiet. I have often seen a little creature, lying in its crib, cooing, laughing, crooning to itself in the sweetest baby fashion, without a care in the world to vex its composure, when in would come mama or nurse, seize it, cover it with endearments and effectually break up its tranquillity. Then, the next time, when these thoughtless people wanted it to be quiet, they were surprised that it refused to be so.

—*Margaret Sangster.*

The Month of

December First

The King of Kings, when He was born,
  Had not so much for outward ease;
By Him such dressings were not worn,
  Nor such-like swaddling clothes as these.
Sweet baby, then, forbear to weep;
  Be still, my babe: sweet baby, sleep.

Within a manger lodged thy Lord,
  Where oxen lay, and asses fed:
Warm rooms we do thee afford,
  An easy cradle for a bed.
Sweet baby, then, forbear to weep,
  Be still, my babe; sweet baby, sleep.

—*George Wither.*

December Second

Most mothers, thank God, have the right *instincts*, but the right insight is, alas! too often lacking. The results in their children's lives that ought to be produced they see clearly, but how to produce these results they have but little idea. A new science is developing among us, which we may call the Science of Motherhood.

—*Hannah Whitall Smith.*

December Third

There was carried out one that was dead, the only son of his mother, and she was a widow. And when the Lord saw her, He had compassion on her, and said unto her, weep not.

—*Luke 7 : 12, 13.*

"Mother of God," some hope I find
  In that remembered word.
Thou, on whose heart the sweet child lay
  Who brought thy heart the sorrow,
Didst thou not see my little son?
  Didst thou not smile to greet him?
With kisses on thy mouth didst run
  To welcome him and greet him?

—*W. J. Dawson.*

December Fourth

Children as individuals do not like to be judged or condemned because they belong to a class, any better than the convict, the Indian, the Chinaman, the Russian Jew, or the negro does. A child feels that he has a place in humanity as well as in childhood.

—*Patterson Du Bois.*

December Fifth

If the Lord should come in the morning
  As I went about my work,
The little things and the quiet things
  That a servant cannot shirk,
Though nobody ever sees them,
  And only the dear Lord cares
That they always are done in the light of the sun,
  Would He take me unawares?

Why do I ask the question?
  He is ever coming to me,
Morning and noon and evening,
  If I have but eyes to see.
And the daily load grows lighter,
  The daily cares grow sweet,
For the Master is near, the Master is here,
  I have only to sit at His feet.

—*Margaret Sangster.*

⚜

December Sixth

A house is built of bricks and stones,
　Of sills and posts and piers;
But a home is built of loving deeds
　That stand a thousand years.
A house though but a humble cot,
　Within its walls may hold
A home of priceless beauty, rich
　In Love's eternal gold.

The men of earth build houses,
　Halls and chambers, roofs and domes—
But the women of the earth, God knows!
　The women build the homes.
Eve could not stray from Paradise,
　For oh! No matter where
Her gracious presence lit the way,
　Lo! Paradise was there.

—*Selectea.*

December Seventh

The atmosphere around the cradle must be serene and placid, the voices of those who speak in the hearing of those tiny ears must be sweet and soothing, and the hands that serve the needs of this helpless creature must be gentle and caressing. The baby cannot understand words, but it can feel the vibrations of sound, it can be impressed by the mental atmosphere, it can be influenced by the manner in which it is handled.

—Mary Wood-Allen.

December Eighth

Yes! Thou art what Thou seemst to be,
  A thing of smiles and tears;
Yet Thou art God, and heaven and earth
  Adore Thee with their fears.

Yes! dearest Babe! those tiny hands,
  That play with Mary's hair,
The weight of all the mighty world
  This very moment bear.

—Frederick W. Faber.

December Ninth

How often parents can trace in the sins and evil tempers of their children, their own shortcomings and transgressions. How the remembrance that their children have inherited their evil natures from themselves ought to humble them, make them so very patient and gentle as well as very earnest and wise.

—*Andrew Murray.*

December Tenth

'Tis a mother's large affection
    Hears with a mysterious sense
Breathings that escape detection,
Whisper faint and fine inflection
    Thrill in her with power intense.
Childhood's honeyed words untaught
Giveth she in loving thought,
Tones that never thence depart,
For she listens—with her heart.

—*Laman Blanchard.*

December Eleventh

A mother dreads no memories,—those shadows have all melted away in the dawn of baby's smiles.

—*George Eliot.*

Child of my heart, lying under my heart, with my relationship to you has grown a new relationship to your father; he is more than lover, husband and king,—high priest of the Most High; love has become sacred and holy beyond words, almost beyond thought.

—*Ellis Meredith.*

⚜

December Twelfth

Two things which should not be; a child without a home; a home without a child.

No piled-up wealth, no splendour of material growth, no brilliance of artistic development, will permanently avail any people unless its home-life is healthy, unless the average man possesses honesty, courage, common sense and decency, unless he works hard and is willing at need to fight hard, and unless the average woman is a good wife, a good mother, able and willing to bear and to bring up as they should be brought up healthy children, sound in body, mind and character, and numerous enough so that the race shall increase and not decrease.

—*Theodore Roosevelt.*

December Thirteenth

Children are poor men's riches.

—*French Proverb.*

The care of little children is always committed to angelic guardianship, as the Lord Himself testifies. Hence, he who has children within his house may be certain that he has therein the presence of angels; he who takes little children in his arms may be assured that he takes angels; whosoever surrounded with midnight darkness rests beside an infant, may enjoy the certain consolation that with it he is so protected that the spirit of darkness cannot have access. How great the importance of these things!

—*Johann Comenius.*

December Fourteenth

Oh! my heart grows weak as a woman's,
  And the fountain of feeling will flow,
When I think of the paths steep and stony,
  Where the feet of the dear ones must go,
Of the mountains of sin hanging o'er them,
  Of the tempest of fate blowing wild!
Oh! there is nothing on earth half so holy
  As the innocent heart of a child.

—*Charles M. Dickenson.*

December Fifteenth

A mother's love, how sweet the name!
  What is a mother's love?
A noble, pure, and tender flame,
  Enkindled from above,
To bless a heart of earthly mould,
The warmest love that can grow cold;
  This is a mother's love.

—*James Montgomery.*

To Adam, Paradise was home. To the good among his descendants, home is paradise.

—*Henry Ware.*

December Sixteenth

A mother has a sacred claim on the world; even if that claim rests solely on the fact of her motherhood, and not, alas, on any other. Her life may be a cipher, but when the child comes, God writes a figure before it, and gives it value.

—*Kate D. Wiggin.*

It is the surrender of faith that makes a blessed motherhood. "Blessed art thou and blessed is the fruit of thy womb."

—*Andrew Murray.*

December Seventeenth

God is so good, He wears a fold
  Of heaven and earth across His face,
Like secrets kept for love untold.

But still I feel that His embrace
  Slides down by thrills through all things made,
Through sight and sound of every place.

As if my tender mother laid
  On my shut lids her kisses' pressure,
Half waking me at night, and said,
  "Who kissed you through the dark, dear guesser?"

—*Elizabeth Barrett Browning.*

December Eighteenth

We thrust our children out of the covenant first, and insist, in spite of it, that they shall grow up in the same spiritual state as if their father and mother were heathen. Then we go out, at least on certain occasions, to convert them back, as if they were actually heathen. The church is gathered as a foundling hospital.

—*Horace Bushnell.*

December Nineteenth

All day the children's busy feet
  Had pattered to and fro;
And all the day their little hands
  Had been in mischief so;—

That oft my patience had been tried;
  But tender, loving care
Had kept them through the day from harm,
  And safe from ev'ry snare.

But when the eventide had come,
  The children went up-stairs,
And knelt beside their little beds,
  To say their wonted prayers.

*   *   *   *   *   *

And as I picked the playthings up,
  And put the books away,
My heart gave grateful thanks to God
  For His kind care all day.

—*Anonymous.*

December Twentieth

Unless thou canst undergo, not in resignation, but in joy and hope, all these months of doubt and anxiety and pain, then know it is not love that knocks at thy heart's door. The woman who does not feel not merely ready, but anxious, to go through the Valley of the Shadow in faith and triumph, does not really love. Until a woman wants to be all that woman can be to man, to lose her life for his, if need be, she may be sure the real king has not come.

—*Ellis Meredith.*

December Twenty-first

Ah! what is it we prize so
  In the little children's kiss?
Something that we long for, strive for,
  Something that so many miss.
Higher, better than this earth is,
  Purer, sweeter, far above
Every other gift that's sent us
  From the realm which we call Love.

—*Minnette McElheny.*

December Twenty-second

And the angel came in unto her and said, Hail, thou that art highly favoured; the Lord is with thee; blessed are thou among women. Fear not, Mary, for thou hast found favour with God. And behold, thou shalt conceive in thy womb and bring forth a son, and thou shalt call His name Jesus. . . . The Holy Ghost shall come upon thee and the power of the Highest shall overshadow thee; therefore also that holy thing which shall be born of thee shall be called the Son of God.

—Luke 1 : 28, 30, 31, 35.

The expectant mother knows herself to be like the angels, one of His servants, doing His commandments, hearkening unto the voice of His Word.

—Andrew Murray.

December Twenty-third

And, thro' all His wondrous childhood,
He would honour and obey,
Love and watch the lowly maiden
In whose gentle arms He lay;
Christian children all must be
Mild, obedient, good as He.

—Cecil F. Alexander.

December Twenty-fourth

And so it was, that, while they were there, the days were accomplished that she should be delivered. And she brought forth her first-born son, and wrapped him in swaddling clothes and laid him in a manger. . . . And the angel said unto them, Fear not; for, behold, I bring you good tidings of great joy, which shall be to all people. For unto you is born this day in the City of David, a Saviour, which is Christ the Lord! —*Luke 2: 6–11.*

God bless the little stockings
All over the land to-night,
Hung in the choicest corners
In a glow of crimson light!

—*Mary Riley Smith.*

December Twenty-fifth

God rest ye, little children, let nothing you affright,
For Jesus Christ, your Saviour, was born this happy night;
Along the hills of Galilee the white flocks sleeping lay,
When Christ, the Child of Nazareth, was born on Christmas day. —*Dinah M. Muloch.*

Christmas day is a time to think of what the coming of a Child to this earth may mean. "And His name shall be called Wonderful." Never a day goes by that I do not think of you as just that. "Wonderful" that you should be ours, lent us to complete our lives. —*Ellis Meredith.*

December Twenty-sixth

Donald, his arms around his mother's neck, laid the little silver saint against her cheek. "Oh, mamma," he cried, his lips touching her ear, "it's yours, for you! Santa Claus did truly bring it to you. For my own love was Santa Claus, wasn't it?"

And then the mother-love, divining all at once the long misery, realizing the faith that had been lost in the faith that was restored, whispered, "That's what love is at Christmas, dear. For Christmas' love is Santa Claus himself."

—*Kathryn Jarboe.*

December Twenty-seventh

The Mexicans whisper over the cradle of a new-born babe, "Child, thou art born to suffer; endure and hold thy peace."

—*J. R. Miller.*

Children, obey your parents in the Lord; for this is right. Honour thy father and mother, which is the first commandment with promise; that it may be well with thee and thou mayest live long on the earth.

And ye, fathers, provoke not your children to wrath, but bring them up in the nurture and admonition of the Lord.

—*Saint Paul.*

December Twenty-eighth

Children,—ninety-nine one-hundredths of those I've seen, at least,—are treated as necessary nuisances by their parents. The good fathers and mothers would be horrified to realize this truth. And when it accidentally presents itself,—as it frequently does to any one with heart and head,—its appearance is so unpleasing and perplexing that they promptly take refuge in tradition. Weren't they brought up in the same way? To be sure, it's the appreciation of the same rule that has always made the ex-slave the cruelest of overseers and the ex-servant the worst of masters; but such comparisons are odious to one's pride, and what chance has self-respect when pride steps down before it?

—*John Habberton.*

December Twenty-ninth

Sometimes, in quiet mood, I fancy, He
Sweet confidence told at Mary's knee.
There childish griefs, if such He had, grew less,
Or, fading out, made room for happiness.
He loved her much, and told her often, too;
And she? She pressed Him close, as mothers do.

December Thirtieth

Blessed is she that believed. And Mary said, My soul doth magnify the Lord:

And my spirit hath rejoiced in God my Saviour:
For He hath regarded the low estate of His
handmaiden, . . .
For He that is mighty hath done to me great
things;
And holy is His name.
And His mercy is unto generations and gen-
erations
On them that fear Him.

—Luke 1 : 45–50.

Around the throne of God in heaven,
Thousands of children stand,
Children whose sins are all forgiven,
A holy, happy band,
Singing, "Glory be to God on High!"

—Anne H. Shepherd.

December Thirty-first

Yesterday now is a part of forever;
  Bound up in a sheaf which God holds tight,
With glad days and sad days and bad days which never
  Shall visit us more with their bloom and their blight,
  Their fullness of sunshine or sorrowful night.

Every day is a fresh beginning;
  Listen, my soul, to the glad refrain,
And in spite of old sorrow and older sinning,
  And puzzles forecasted and possibly pain,
  Take heart with the day and begin again.

—*Susan Coolidge.*

INDEX OF AUTHORS